Your
Psychic
Self

About the Author

Melissa Alvarez lives in Juno Beach, Florida, and is an internationally known spiritual coach and an award-winning author. She conducts workshops teaching others to connect with their psychic abilities and spirituality, and has performed psychic readings for nearly twenty years.

To Write to the Author

If you wish to contact the author or would like more information about this book, please write to the author in care of Llewellyn Worldwide, and we will forward your request. Both the author and publisher appreciate hearing from you and learning of your enjoyment of this book and how it has helped you. Llewellyn Worldwide cannot guarantee that every letter written to the author can be answered, but all will be forwarded. Please write to:

Melissa Alvarez
℅ Llewellyn Worldwide
2143 Wooddale Drive
Woodbury, MN 55125-2989
Please enclose a self-addressed stamped envelope for reply,
or $1.00 to cover costs. If outside the USA, enclose
an international postal reply coupon.

Many of Llewellyn's authors have websites with additional information and resources. For more information, please visit our website at http://www.llewellyn.com.

Praise for
Your Psychic Self:

"This comprehensive reference book contains excellent information to help anyone—regardless of their degree of expertise—to recognize, enhance, harness, and clarify their intuitive abilities. It's an exceptionally diverse, detailed, and accessible guide to the various forms of psychic impressions, techniques, and challenges. (And I can't wait to try out Melissa's unique approach to intuitively handling a crowd!)"

—Tess Whitehurst, author of
The Good Energy Book and *The Art of Bliss*

"Our sixth sense, the gift of intuition, is becoming available to everyone. As this new awareness develops, it's helpful to have a guide to understand how to discern, connect and harness this new power. Melissa Alvarez's new book, *Your Psychic Self: A Quick and Easy Guide to Discovering Your Intuitive Talent,* explains how to connect with these abilities while maintaining a grounded and centered core. A wonderful twenty-first century guide to exploring our intuitive evolution."

—Kala Ambrose, oracle, host of Explore Your Spirit with Kala
and author of *The Awakened Aura:*
Experiencing the Evolution of Your Energy Body

"From Auras to Runes, Spirit Guides to Orbs, this book covers all aspects of intuitive abilities. Perfect for the inquisitive beginner."

—Elizabeth Owens, author of
Spiritualism and Clairvoyance for Beginners

"Melissa Alvarez shares a simple yet complete approach to developing your psychic abilities, making *Your Psychic Self* a fun and practical addition to your library!"

—Melanie Barnum, author of
The Book of Psychic Symbols: Interpreting Intuitive Messages

Praise for
365 Ways to Raise Your Frequency:

"365 Ways to Raise Your Frequency presents an eclectic and insightful perspective on the many ways we can connect to our core spiritual essence by raising our vibration emotionally, physically, mentally, and spiritually. Some primary keys to success are to practice, trust, and believe in your inner self."

—Dawn James, author of
Raise Your Vibration, Transform Your Life

"I am always on the lookout for other modalities that I can segue into my work with tarot. Melissa Alvarez has given me exactly what I need and 365 ways to do it. Deceptively simple, this book can help you on your own path."

—Stephanie Arwen Lynch,
professional Tarot consultant and reader

"A must-read for everyone who wants to move forward on the path of life. Melissa Alvarez has given us a daily road map for achieving happiness and success through simply shifting our vibrations, with 365 engaging methods of doing so. Brilliant and highly recommended for all!"

—Dyan Garris, author and New Age musician

Melissa Alvarez

Your
Psychic
Self

A Quick and Easy Guide to
Discovering Your Intuitive Talents

Llewellyn Publications
Woodbury, Minnesota

FIRST EDITION
Eighth Printing, 2019

Book design by Bob Gaul
Cover art: Background © iStockphoto.com /Amanda Rohde
Cover design by Lisa Novak
Editing by Amy Quale

Llewellyn Publications is a registered trademark of Llewellyn Worldwide Ltd.

Library of Congress Cataloging-in-Publication Data
Alvarez, Melissa.
  Your psychic self: a quick and easy guide to discovering your intuitive talents/
Melissa Alvarez.—1st ed.
      p. cm.
  Includes bibliographical references.
  ISBN 978-0-7387-3189-6
1. Psychic ability. 2. Intuition—Miscellanea. I. Title.
  BF1031.A46 2013
  133.8—dc23
                            2012040511

Llewellyn Worldwide Ltd. does not participate in, endorse, or have any authority or responsibility concerning private business transactions between our authors and the public.

All mail addressed to the author is forwarded, but the publisher cannot, unless specifically instructed by the author, give out an address or phone number.

Any Internet references contained in this work are current at publication time, but the publisher cannot guarantee that a specific location will continue to be maintained. Please refer to the publisher's website for links to authors' websites and other sources.

Llewellyn Publications
A Division of Llewellyn Worldwide Ltd.
2143 Wooddale Drive
Woodbury, MN 55125-2989
www.llewellyn.com

Printed in the United States of America

Disclaimer

1. There is a difference between intuitive impressions and mental disease. If you are hearing voices and believe these voices are going to hurt you, seek professional medical attention and consult with a doctor to rule out any type of mental illness, as your experience may not be intuitive in nature. The author is not a doctor and does not give medical advice.

2. The examples shared with you in this book are the author's personal experiences. Your experiences may be similar to or completely different from these examples. The way the author experiences psychic abilities and intuition is based on personal beliefs and interpretations, just as your psychic abilities are based upon your own personal beliefs and interpretations. This book is intended to be a guide to psychic abilities, not the final word on the subject.

This book is dedicated to my husband Jorge for his unwavering belief in me, constant support, and unconditional love.

Acknowledgments

I wish to express my most heartfelt appreciation for those who have traveled this life path with me, to those who have assisted me during the publication of both this book and my previous title with Llewellyn Worldwide, *365 Ways to Raise Your Frequency*, and to family and friends whose belief in me often surpassed my belief in myself.

I would like to thank those on the spiritual realm for their assistance: To God for giving me these abilities and the task of teaching; I've sometimes floundered along the way and I am still learning every day as I travel this path to bring light into the world. To my spirit guides, Cassandra, Ally, and Robert, for watching over me, for making me see when I closed my eyes and ignored my abilities, and for teaching me how to become one with my true spiritual essence. To my angels, for your guidance and for keeping me safely out of danger on more than one occasion.

To my family: my husband Jorge and sons Jorgie, Jordan, Jason, and Justin; I wouldn't be me without you. God truly blessed me with a wonderful, loving family. You mean more to me than words can ever express. You are my light, my love, and my heart. Thank you for understanding when I'm stressed due to deadlines, sick animals, or when I simply have too much on my plate. You've taught me patience and unconditional love, and you continue to amaze me. You're the best husband and sons in the world. I love you all forever and through eternity.

To my mama, Nancy: You have believed in me always, you have lifted me up when I was down, hugged me while I cried, and been a beacon of light when I doubted. You taught me to go after what I wanted and to believe in myself even when the things I said were difficult to believe. Thank you for being such a special and important person in my life. I love you!

To my daddy, Warren: Your philosophical and logical advice has always kept me moving forward. I'll never forget that the shortest distance between two points is a straight line. Thank you for buying Lady for me when my savings wasn't enough, for giving me a Mustang for my first car and teaching me how to fix it, for believing in Mac, and for all the silly bantering and funny voices. You taught me to stand up for myself when the going got rough, and you kept me grounded. You're the best daddy a girl could hope for. I love you!

To my brothers, Vincent, Brian, Eric, and Scott: I love you all even when we don't see eye to eye. And yes, I do believe in all the things I write about in these books!

To my mother-in-law, Zenaida: Thank you for embracing me into your family, for all of your support and love throughout the years, and for teaching me Spanish and how to cook Cuban food.

To Momo, Pat, Michael, Momo Mac, and Mac: For sending me signs and showing me without a doubt that there is life after death. One day we'll be together again. I love you all.

To the rest of my huge extended family, all of my in-laws, cousins, uncles, and aunts: Thank you all for being part of my life. They say you can't help the family you were born or married into, and I'm blessed to be part of a wonderful group of people. We may not get to see each other very often, so just remember how much I love you.

To Aunt Jo: Thank you for always reading my books.

To Aunt Sugar Pie: Thank you for believing in my psychic abilities and telling others that you do!

To Dyan Garris: Thank you for so graciously writing the foreword to this book. You are an exceptionally gifted spiritual and psychic person, with your own mission to teach through VoiceoftheAngels.com, and I'm honored that you offered to support me in this way. Your kindness and friendship mean the world to me.

To all my psychic friends: There are too many of you to name individually and I'd hate to inadvertently leave someone out, but you all know who you are! Thank you for discussing psychic abilities, the paranormal, metaphysics and spirituality, animals, publishing, and life in general with me, for asking questions that made me dig deeper within my essence and my abilities to find the answers, for trusting in my abilities, and for giving me a reading when I was unsure about something. I always say that everything happens for a reason and each and every one of you has a specific reason for being in my life. I am truly honored and blessed to know and be friends with all of you.

To the staff at Llewellyn Worldwide: Carrie Obry, my former editor, thank you for suggesting that I turn one chapter into a full-length book. You saw a spark in my writing and for that I'm eternally grateful. To Angela Wix, my current editor, thank you for being there when I needed you, for answering questions promptly, and for offering valuable suggestions. To my production editors, thank you for making my work shine. To the staff who work behind the scenes, thank you for the great covers and wonderful publicity. To everyone who has worked so hard on my behalf to bring my words to the world, thank you from the bottom of my heart.

To my many clients and workshop attendees, who have come to me over the years to gain clarity in their lives: you have shared your fears, hopes, and joys; you have asked metaphysical questions; and you took the time to let me know that I was able to help and make a difference in your lives. For those of you who sought me out after having horrific experiences with people who instilled fear within you, thank you for your trust. I give you my sincerest gratitude for your belief in me. You are the reason I continue on this path. I thank you all for enriching my life. You have each touched me on a very personal level and for that I am grateful. Helping you is the reason I continue to do this work. I appreciate all of you.

And finally, thank you to the many animals that are, or have been, part of my life. You have each blessed me with unconditional love and taught me many lessons about life. I couldn't leave you out. I love you all.

Contents

Five: Using Your Abilities in Everyday Life   81

Seven: Types of Readers/Readings/Spirit Beings   147

Eight: Types of Intuitive Communication   187

Nine: Protecting Yourself from Negative Situations   201

Ten: Where Do You Go from Here?   217

Foreword

You find yourself finishing someone's sentences before they've finished speaking, yet you don't even know that person. The phone rings and you know who is calling without glancing at the Caller ID. You sometimes hear things. Lately, you even smell things that aren't anywhere near you—the pungent aroma of fresh oranges, the delicate yet distinct fragrance of blooming roses. You just know things. Are you an anomaly? Far from it!

As the veils continue to thin between our world and other dimensions, many people are now experiencing psychic phenomena more than ever before. They are having what can only be described as "psychic experiences." But does having psychic experiences mean that you are psychic? Is everyone psychic? And most importantly, what are we supposed to do with these experiences and abilities?

If we believe that we were dropped off on the planet with no way to communicate with anyone or anything other than ourselves, then our emerging psychic abilities and seeming plethora of psychic experiences would perhaps seem bizarre. However, that is not the case. We arrived here with an intrinsic sense of who we are. We are not alone. You are not alone. Just as a child will eventually become an adult, we move forward now toward maturity through the somewhat foggy swirling mists of all we have created on Earth. And so, as we evolve, change, shift, and transform, our eyes open and we see clearly that maturity walks with responsibility on the path to enlightenment. As such, we have a responsibility to embrace not only ourselves and each other, but also those entities that communicate with us from unseen realms.

It is essential that we learn to recognize, understand, and develop our innate psychic gifts, not as something to be feared or misunderstood, but as something wonderful to be welcomed, honored, and embraced like an esteemed family member. When we do this, we raise our frequency not only as individuals, but also as a collective global consciousness. And that is what propels us forward toward our inevitable ascension.

It is time to become all we can be so that we may help one another on this journey. It is time to fully accept our innate gifts as the blessings they are. All signs point clearly to that. *Your Psychic Self* opens the door not to the trickster's abode of yesteryear, but to a more solid foundation and to the deeply spiritual place that inherently exists within all of us. And when you've discovered these signs, you will find that even more will be revealed to you—you will discover your true and infinite connection to all that is.

—Dyan Garris, psychic medium, author,
and New Age recording artist

Introduction

If you've ever experienced something strange, weird, or out of the ordinary, you might be wondering if you have intuitive abilities. If so, are you trying to discover your unique abilities or expand your knowledge of the metaphysical world? Everyone who has acknowledged their abilities has asked themselves questions at some point along their path of spiritual growth.

Many people are seeking out spiritual advisors for guidance as they try to understand their lives in the modern world while on a quest for their own spiritual growth and enlightenment through the understanding of universal laws. People are seeking a mind-body-spirit connection; they are intrigued by the possibilities of the unknown, what happens to us after death, and if we've lived before. Even if you haven't experienced an intuitive, metaphysical, or paranormal event yourself, you probably know someone who has or you've seen programs about it on television. There are many documentaries that feature intuitives helping the police solve crimes and mediums bringing comfort to those left behind. Viewers have proven that their interest in the Other Side is not just a passing fancy. The Universal knowledge is out there waiting for each of us to embrace it and make it our own. Once we do, we can use it to enrich lives and acquire a deeper understanding of the spiritual self.

It is my opinion that we all have different truths based on where we are on our path of spiritual enlightenment and that our knowledge is attained through individual experiences. To me, psychic abilities and spirituality go hand in hand. They're intricately wound together and both exist simultaneously. In this book, I discuss both of these topics together to show you how connected they are, which I hope aids in the development of your own abilities and connection to your own spirituality. My experiences and the ways my abilities operate may be similar to your experiences or completely different. It is my hope that relaying what I've learned will help you travel your own path. By sharing my truths and experiences, I might strike a chord in you, and in some small way, I might help you gain a clearer understanding of these topics while teaching you how to further expand your abilities. My slogan has always been "gain clarity in your life," and I hope that this book will enable you to do just that.

When I realized that I was different, even though I didn't know what to call my abilities at the time, I felt very alone. I didn't understand what was going on and why I experienced the things that I did. Quite frankly, as a child I was scared to death of the things I saw, especially at night. The older I got, the more I researched and found out the meanings behind my strange experiences. In my twenties, I delved even deeper and began to study the metaphysical in earnest. I found a lot of helpful information, but I still wished I had someone in my life who understood what I was going through—someone I could talk to about what was happening because they had encountered the same types of experiences.

After years of honing my abilities to make sure that I understood them myself, and could indeed help others understand what they were going through, I decided to offer my services as a mentor, which meant one-on-one unlimited e-mail exchanges with me twenty-four/seven for one month. I really enjoy helping people understand their abilities, but I was soon overwhelmed with mentoring requests and didn't have enough time in the day to help everyone. As an author, I decided that it was time to write a book that would serve to mentor others on psychic development, and in subject matters that are considered "New Age" (which I also categorize as metaphysical in nature) that would help them understand and develop their own intuitive abilities. That was the catalyst behind this book. There are many reasons this book is important, but there is one reason that tops them all: when someone reads about a metaphysical event experienced by someone else, it may validate their own experiences. I wish I'd had a book when I was growing up to read about others' experiences, or a mentor who could have enlightened me along the way.

Knowledge is power. The truth will set you free. I can't think of any area where these two thoughts apply more than in psychic and spiritual development. As the curious delve deeper into the unknown and those who live it share their experiences, doorways to greater understanding are opened. Gaining knowledge of New Age metaphysics and different types of intuitive and metaphysical events can be very empowering. I'll say it again—knowledge is power—and it's *your* truth that will set you upon the path of spiritual growth and your own enlightenment.

We are all spiritual beings who have the ability to develop our intuitive awareness and attune ourselves with the Other Side. Some of us choose not to do so because it can be a little unnerving to face the unknown; for others, it's simply not their path in this lifetime. Some people, like me, find that these intuitive and metaphysical events are part of everyday life, and regardless of how much we fight it, ignore it, or hope it goes away, it doesn't. Once we embrace all aspects of ourselves, life is easier, fuller, and more peaceful.

Why is it that some people can see things others can't? What gives them the ability to just "know"? By way of introduction, I thought I would tell you a little bit about my abilities, how I got them, and how they affected me as I learned to deal with them.

I discovered my psychic abilities at the age of fourteen. I experienced a sudden illness, very much like the flu but different because I was unable to raise my head from my pillow without feeling intense pain. The doctor could only tell us what I didn't have, not the actual cause of the illness. The morning that I became ill, I saw an elemental spirit that told me that I would get very ill and afterward I would be able to "know" things. At the time, I thought I was hallucinating. As soon as the elemental spirit disappeared, everything happened just as I was told. I was extremely ill for more than two weeks. My parents took me to several doctors and none could determine the cause of my illness. Shortly after my recovery, I did indeed begin to "know" things. At first it was very scary for me, a fourteen-year-old girl, because I couldn't explain how I knew things or why I would see spirits passing by or why my dreams started to come true. I have since found out that intuitive abilities run on both sides of my family and go back many generations. The illness just brought out the abilities that I'd had since birth.

The following summer, I was helping my father and he sent me to get an electrical tool from the basement of my grandparents' house, which was next door to our house. It was summertime, so naturally I was bare-foot. My grandparents' basement was unfinished and had a cement floor. I found the tool at the base of the stairs but it was plugged into the wall on the opposite side of the basement. As I walked over, I noticed that there were two electrical cords connected, so instead of walking the rest of the way to unplug it from the wall, I just unplugged the two cords. Big mistake! Because I was barefoot and standing on concrete, the current ran right through me somehow. I couldn't move, I couldn't speak, I could only stand there making some weird noises and shaking. My grandfather had been in the kitchen and heard something happening and came running downstairs to see what was wrong. He was a police officer and wore these big brown shoes with thick rubber soles. I remember everything happening in slow motion as he grabbed each of the cords and yanked them out of my hands, which sent yellow and red sparks flying into the air, then he pulled really hard on the cord still plugged into the wall and yanked it out of the socket. He caught me as I collapsed. If he hadn't been in the kitchen, which was at the top of the stairs to the basement, and heard what was happening downstairs, I'm pretty sure I would have died that day. I don't remember anything else from the time that he caught me until I woke up lying on my bed with everyone standing around staring at me with strange looks on their faces. I found out later that a doctor who lived nearby had come by to examine me and left after telling my family that I'd be okay. The strange looks were because I'd been sleeping with my eyes open and my family was afraid because I looked dead. That day I learned some very important lessons: always unplug things from the wall and never, ever unplug something when you're barefoot and standing on cement.

As an adult I've heard of many other peoples' experiences where electricity brought out their intuitive abilities. I believe this near-electrocution strengthened the abilities I was born with even more. Why does electricity do this? I'm not sure, but I believe such high levels of energy flowing through our human body charges up our cells and spirit so that we attune to a higher level of frequency, thereby enabling us to connect to inner latent abilities.

I wasn't taught about being intuitive while growing up and had to learn about intuitive abilities on my own as they manifested in my life. I tried to ignore them and hoped they'd go away—but of course, they didn't. Since the early days of my abilities, I've come to understand that none of our abilities ever truly goes away. We can choose not to use them or even recognize them, but they stay dormant within us, just in case we ever change our minds and decide to embrace them.

This book is designed to help you recognize how your abilities can manifest in your daily life so that when you have intuitive or metaphysical experiences, you'll recognize them. Whether you're just beginning to investigate and understand your spiritual self or are fully aware and comfortable with your intuitive nature, this book can be a tool to deepen your understanding.

When describing these abilities, one may use the terms "intuitive" or "psychic." Exactly what does the word "psychic" mean? The Online Etymology Dictionary (etymonline.com) defines *psychic* as "pertaining to the human soul or mind; mental phenomena outside of natural or scientific knowledge; spiritual; pertaining to some apparently nonphysical force or agency; sensitive to influences or forces of a nonphysical or supernatural nature; a person who is allegedly sensitive to psychic influences or forces; medium." All of these definitions are true, but if you want to know specifically what it means to have psychic or intuitive abilities, you have to look deeper into each type of ability to find out how it manifests and then determine if you have that ability. Psychic abilities tend to be unpredictable; they happen when you don't want them to, and when you want them to work, they may refuse to cooperate. As you develop and grow in your abilities this will happen less often.

Over the years, I've found that there are many different variations of what is considered "normal" when it comes to intuitive abilities. In fact, there are as many variations of normalcy as there are people on the planet. As individuals, we will each have subtle differences in the ways our abilities manifest. One person may only have clairaudience while another has all of the "clair" abilities intertwined and uses all of them at the same time. Both are normal and right for each individual; it doesn't make one person more or less intuitive than the other because one has multiple abilities. Both are intuitive, just in different ways. Strength of abilities also varies in intensity. Sometimes the presentation is so slight that, had you not been paying attention, you may have missed it. Other times it is so intense there is no doubt something metaphysical just happened. Some people have abilities that are so ingrained in their being that if the abilities were suddenly taken away, the person would feel lost. Many people are accustomed to their abilities and use them daily, even if they don't consider them to be psychic abilities.

Abilities often work hand in hand with each other. While you may see something happen, you can also hear words that help you understand what you're seeing or you may simply know more information about the situation as you watch it unfold. Abilities will often work together in order to give you an impression you can use to help someone else, or to give you an answer to a question or situation you are encountering in your own life.

There is a broad range of intuitive abilities that are widely known and have specific names. In this book I've given you many examples of these abilities that will include:

1. Definitions and examples of well-known terms for different types of abilities.

2. Ways those abilities present themselves in your daily life.

3. Situations where you may use your ability.

4. Examples and methods from my own life that will teach you how to enhance your own intuitive nature.

The information is organized so that you can start at the beginning and read through until the end with each item building upon the previous one. If you have a particular interest, you can choose to skip ahead to that section.

As you walk this path, it's important to remember that your abilities are gifts. You are the guardian of your own abilities and it's up to you to use them in a positive manner. Even though you're researching and learning, when it comes right down to it, you already know the truth of your abilities on a soul level. It is the connection to your soul truth that lets you know that what you are seeing, feeling, sensing, and experiencing is really intuitive—when it's your imagination. When it is intuitive, it will touch a chord within you. When you are connected to your soul truth, there will be no doubt. If you don't feel this connection, you should probably do more spiritual work until you're able to tell the difference. These abilities are part of your spiritual truth and your life path. It is also important to understand yourself; this means you have a deep sense of your true soul essence—the true nature of your being on a soul level—and your abilities. Then you can make the choices that are right for you as you become more enlightened, and that will bring about the most spiritual growth, psychic development, and healing.

To me, spirituality, psychic abilities, and the total mind-body-spirit experience are so intricately intertwined as part of our true soul essence that they can't really be separated one from another. The more you can understand or relate to these intricacies, the more you will understand your spiritual self. What you're experiencing is unique to you and is part of your growth. If you look around, you will find plenty of like-minded individuals who understand the path you're on and who will offer you support and love along the way. You are unique. Embrace your uniqueness.

It's also imperative to remember that subtleties are important when it comes to your abilities. We all had to start somewhere along the edge of discovery and grow to the point where we can share our knowledge with the world. This is a lifelong journey. You were born with your intuitive abilities, and while it may take an event to bring these abilities to the forefront, once you recognize them and practice using them the more accurate you will be. However, you will always experience times when your impressions are wrong. You're not always going to have huge psychic epiphanies, but will more often than not have little subtle things that occur as a wandering thought or you notice something that you see every day in a different light. Sometimes a whisper can be more power-ful than a shout. It's the same way with your abilities. Subtleties hold a lot of power. Anytime you're picking up information from outside of yourself, your knowledge or experiences that you normally wouldn't know, you're exercising your intuitive abilities.

In the past I've known people who would try to "will" themselves to have specific abilities. Be careful of trying too hard or forcing your abili-ties because that's oftentimes when you inadvertently block yourself. With intuition, either it's working for you or it's not. When you try to force your abilities to work instead of allowing it to happen naturally, then how do you know it's truly intuition and not your imagination at work? It's better to let your abilities develop gradually and fine-tune them through practice rather than trying to force them to happen before you're ready.

I've always told people to research and read as much as they can about intuitive abilities, the paranormal, and spirituality in order to become more enlightened. Research is valuable because reading how someone else felt or experienced something may hit home with you. I've also always said that you should take what feels right to you, what strikes a chord deep within you on a soul level as a "Universal Truth," and embrace it. If what you're researching doesn't feel right to you, then discard it. It could be that you're not yet ready to learn that lesson, or it might not be applicable to you in this lifetime. When you're ready and the time is right, in the present life or another, the information will come back around to you. When information strikes you as truth, embrace it at that time.

As you work on your intuitive development, stay balanced and grounded in your reality, and appreciate the subtle instances of the metaphysical within it; however, don't overthink every experience you have or become obsessed with being "psychic," as this will separate you from the lessons you actually need to be learning in the realities of this life, and won't help you to proceed forward in your path. Sometimes a cat hissing is just a cat hissing and not a sign that a spirit is in the room, and paying it too much attention will distract you from the needed lessons in your normal life experience. Also, it is healthy not to take every intuitive or metaphysical experience you have too seriously—know that there's always room for growth, and how you reflect on an intuitive experience now might be much different in ten years because you will have grown in your experiences. Live for the lessons you must learn in the present, and know that the next lessons will come to you when it is time without any forcing on your part. When you're centered and balanced, life flows much better, you have a clearer understanding of yourself and your life plan, and that's more beneficial to you.

Just as we are made up of energy—our own personal frequency— our intuitive abilities are also made of this same energy. We are connecting to pure energy when we receive impressions or messages, see physical manifestations, or hear sounds from the spiritual realms. In order to grow within your own spirituality and develop your abilities to their highest possible state, embrace your inner truths and be comfortable in knowing that your intuitions are coming to you for a reason. Acceptance and faith is as important as believing in yourself, in your abilities, and in your own path. This is your life, your lessons, and your spiritual growth. You are pure energy.

It is my goal to enlighten and empower readers. When you sit down with this book, I hope you feel that we're sitting down together, discussing these topics in the living room on your couch (or mine). I want you to feel that I'm having a discussion with you about my experiences, thoughts, and opinions regarding the metaphysical. In the journey you have before you, know that you can talk with me or ask me a question via my current e-mail on my author website at MelissaA.com. I'd love to hear from you. Whether you are a confirmed "believer" in New Age spirituality or are just curious about metaphysical topics, I hope you enjoy this book as much as I enjoyed writing it.

One

Getting Started

Today, people use the words "metaphysics," "New Age," and "spiritualism" interchangeably when they refer to spirituality, spirits, the paranormal, past lives, or other topics that are beyond the physical world. There are certain fundamental beliefs and tools that go along with these concepts, which can help you to look inward for awareness and an understanding of yourself. Your personal awakening and spiritual growth influences which beliefs you embrace and the tools you use, if any. The point is to gain a higher understanding of ourselves, the Universe, and the Other Side as we gain wisdom, transcend ourselves, and strive to attain the higher good.

In this first chapter, I'm going to give you an overview of some of the basics so that you'll be familiar with them when I mention them later on in the book. If you want more information on any of the topics I'm discussing, I highly recommend that you start your continued research with the titles I've included in the Recommended Reading List at the back of this book.

Does Everyone Have Intuitive Abilities?

Think about this for a moment: did you know when the phone was going to ring, and when it did, you knew who it was before you ever answered? Or maybe you've seen a woman standing in line in the grocery store and you were overwhelmed with grief because you somehow knew that her husband had passed, and moments after this knowledge came to you, the cashier confirmed it by offering the woman her condolences. Are these intuitive abilities or were you just on a "coincidence" roll that day? I'd say you were being clairvoyant and empathic in these two examples.

I believe everyone has intuitive abilities. Some people are more naturally gifted than others, but we all have them. They are commonly referred to as "a mother's intuition," a "gut reaction," or a "sixth sense." It's up to each of us as individuals to decide whether we'll nurture and grow these talents or let them sit dormant within us. You may choose to develop them to the point that you can do readings for others or you may just use them in your daily life and for your own peace of mind. If you would like to tap in to and expand your own intuition, I've put together some exercises within this book that will aid in this process.

As you develop your abilities, always remember that you'll never be 100 percent accurate in your readings. You're not omniscient. Know that you will make mistakes and that sometimes the impressions you see, hear, or feel may be inaccurate because you're only human. Keep track of your experiences by writing them down in a journal so you can look back at them later to see how much you've progressed. I also suggest writing down the results of every exercise in this book, as you do it, for the same reason. You'll know that you're getting better when you get more impressions right than wrong.

Trusting in your impressions is just as important as practicing with your abilities. Instead of letting doubt filter into your mind, see the situation clearly, and then trust that you've seen what you were supposed to see about the event. The more you trust in your abilities, the more accurate they will become. Sometimes what you see takes time to happen. Trusting in your abilities will enable you to wait for the confirmation of your impressions.

Just keep at it; keep practicing, and believe in yourself and your abilities. When you claim them as your own, you'll be amazed at what can happen. There's a reason you're reading this book. Maybe it's time to consider developing your own psychic abilities.

Why Me?

I always say, and firmly believe, that everything happens for a reason, even if we don't know or understand the reason at the time. This is true in every aspect of your life, including your intuition. The first time you have a metaphysical experience, it can bring your current views of the world to a screeching halt if you've never considered these abilities before. The event affects you deeply, on a soul level, because once you've had that first metaphysical experience, you begin to question everything else. What does this mean? Why did it happen to me? What makes me different? Why didn't the other people around me see what I saw? Why, why, why? Suddenly you're a two-year-old again who only wants to know "why?" You're learning that the world is multidimensional, filled with layer upon layer of intuitive, spiritual, and metaphysical concepts and lessons that you'd never even thought about before now.

There are times in all of our lives when good things happen to us and other times when bad things happen, but we sense that there is a higher purpose behind the events or that someone is "behind the scenes" helping us. When you feel this connection, you start to understand the bigger picture of life because you're reconnecting to your soul; your intuitive nature is part of your soul. The emergence of your abilities always happens when you need them. Did your impression keep you or someone you love out of harm's way? Did it open your mind to new possibilities? It is time for you to see past your human existence in this life. The more you learn, the more you will want to learn. You still may not understand every event, but you're trying to see the reason behind it. Sometimes it may take years for you to understand the "why"; other times, you never do. But the fact that a metaphysical event manifested in your life changes you forever.

Embrace your abilities. Practice to make them stronger and more precise. Do the best you can to use your intuitive abilities with intent and to make a positive difference in the world or in someone's life. Then you will be living your soul's purpose. Instead of asking "why me?" try asking "why not me?"

Try It Now: Practice Your Intuition

Here are some practice exercises to get you started. In a later chapter, we'll discuss the different types of abilities. As you do these exercises, remember that it's important to listen to your *first* impression, which is usually right. When you start second-guessing yourself, you'll find your accuracy will drop.

The telephone: Trying to predict who is on the telephone is an excellent way to begin tapping in to your abilities. When the phone rings, don't look at the caller ID, just try to determine who is on the other end of the line before you answer. You can also write down a list of who you think will call you the next day. As they do, check them off of your list. At the end of the day, you'll see how accurate your predictions were. We'll discuss an in-depth exercise about using the telephone in a later chapter.

The television: When watching the news, take note of any stories where you can predict the outcome. Make note of them in your mind or write them down. Then follow the story to see if the outcomes you saw really happen. Also, pick a famous psychic that you feel a connection with and watch them do readings on television. Try to give your answer to the person's question before the psychic does—then compare how many times your answers match.

Flash cards: Use flash cards or even a regular deck of cards to help you develop your abilities and practice with them. Really focus on one card at a time, trying to see a picture of it in your mind's eye. Shuffle the deck, say which card you think it is, and then flip it over to see if you're right. You can also work with someone else; have them shuffle and hold up the cards so that you have no contact with them.

Voice of Your Spirit, Inner Voice, Higher Self

If you've experienced whispered words of encouragement, a subtle warning, or a soft inner voice guiding you through the day, then you are connecting with your inner spirit. You hear the words in your head clearly, as if you said them out loud, yet they seem to come from a source other than your mind. It's different from your analytical voice, which is in a state of constant babble weighing pros and cons, making to-do lists, and thinking about everything that is going on in your life. The words from your inner voice are spoken in a different tone—the voice is softer and gentler, yet it instantly grabs your attention and makes you listen, overriding that babbling analyzer. This is your inner voice, the voice of your spirit. It is part of you, yet it is a vehicle that can also be used by your higher self, angels, spirit guides, and masters to communicate with you on a soul level.

How do you know when the voice is your babbling analyzer and not your higher self? Messages and guidance that come from your spiritual inner voice will be loving, kind, and will oftentimes make you think in a bigger, more Universal way than you normally do. Thoughts that are judgmental, negative, or condescending are coming from your thinking mind, your babbling analyzer. We tend to be really hard on ourselves on this plane of existence. It's only when we can start listening to the spiritual inner voice—and tune out the negative one that keeps putting us down or talking a mile a minute about nothing—that we can truly become one with our own intuitive abilities and spiritual nature. The spiritual inner voice is a helper from within and from beyond. We just have to see it for what it is and understand how to use it to make progress on our journey.

You can do this by asking yourself a question and receiving an answer from your spiritual inner voice. You might even be surprised at how wise the answers are that you receive. This is because you're intuitively connecting at a soul level with your higher self, your spirit guides and masters, who are all at a much higher frequency than you can be on the earthly plane.

How do you connect with your spiritual inner voice? Sometimes you'll just hear it out of the blue when you're not expecting it. These are times when someone from the spiritual realm has an important message that they just can't wait to tell you. Other times, you want to take a moment to seek out your inner voice and ask questions. To do this, close your eyes, take a couple of cleansing breaths, and listen within. Sometimes you'll intuitively hear things that your thinking mind wants to reject. You can listen to your spiritual inner voice all day long, but if you never take positive action on the things you've learned, you're wasting the information you've been given to help you grow. Staying intuitively in tune with your inner voice can open up a wealth of information to you.

Intention

Does your intuitive energy feel like it's all over the place? Or that no matter what you do to develop your ability, to truly understand and use it, nothing ever happens for you or works the way other people say it should? It's great that you're focusing on your abilities because that's how you grow. But are you working on developing your abilities with the right intention? In the years that I've been helping other people develop their psychic ability, I've noticed that often, when things aren't working properly and a person is stuck, it's because they aren't working from within their energy and they're not working with the right level of intention. If you try to force your abilities, you'll dig your tires right into the mud. To develop your ability, you must be clear and intend what you want to happen. To have the purest intention, you have to release any preconceived notions of how your abilities will work; you have to understand that the way you receive information is right for you and be receptive to what happens even if it's unexpected. Your abilities may be totally different from your sibling or best friend. There may be similarities but there are always little differences. Granted, some experiences are going to completely overwhelm you and change your life. They come out of the blue and surprise you. But if you're working toward a specific goal, you should have a specific intention to get you to that goal.

If you want to meet one of your guides, then your intention could be something like, "Through focused effort on my energy, I will find a quiet, still place within my being where I can become one with divine energy. In this place I will ask my guide to come forward and speak with me telepathically, helping me to understand my place in the world and my spiritual existence." That is a very specific intention and will help you to meet your guide. Use your own words to make your intention part of your being. Then, when you connect to your guide in this quiet place, thank your guide for meeting with you and answering your questions.

Clear intention is necessary when trying to understand and develop your intuitive abilities. It can help you be free of fear, find your center, and enable you to be successful as you try new things. Pure intention will allow you to release any negativity you receive from those who don't understand your experiences. You may not even understand them yourself, but by being clear and pure in your intent, you can discover windows when doors shut and phenomena that the logical mind may have trouble explaining.

Visualization

Have you ever had the feeling that someone you know needed you and then shortly thereafter found out that what you'd sensed was true? In situations such as these, you can use visualization to determine if you should take action. Let's say that you get this feeling but you're not sure if it's just your thinking mind or an intuitive impression. Take a moment to visualize that person in the moment. You may see them in a situation where they're upset and need to talk or they may be having dinner, laughing, and talking with friends. Depending on what you visualize, you will know whether you should reach out to them in that moment. Visualization is helpful when you're developing your abilities because it is a method you can use to see further with your abilities. You can use visualization to double-check that what you're sensing is correct.

Creative visualization is different in that you use it to create a specific outcome. For instance, if you're trying to connect with your spirit guides, you can use creative visualization to see yourself meeting your guides, talking with them, and learning from them. You see this as an image or movie in your mind's eye. If you want to enhance your empathic abilities, you can visualize yourself as a more feeling person who is able to sense and understand the feelings of others. Creative visualization is also important in manifesting positive things in your life. If you want to bring more optimistic situations into your life, you imagine that positivity surrounds you—upbeat and positive people, things, and circumstances—and those things will come to you because you are thinking about them with intention and desiring them in your life.

Chakra Balancing

Within your body there are hundreds of chakras that nurture us with Universal Life Force. Among these hundreds of chakras are seven primary ones, which are numbered and named, and are located from the top of your head down to the base of your spine. The seven primary chakras are the crown chakra (seventh) located at the top of your head, the third-eye chakra (sixth) located in the forehead between the eyes, the throat chakra (fifth) located in the neck region, the heart chakra (fourth) located in the center of your chest, the solar-plexus chakra (third) located in the stomach area near the navel, the sacral chakra (second) located in the lower abdomen right below the navel, and the root/base chakra (first) located at the base of the spine near the tailbone.

Each chakra gives your body a specific kind of energy that is essential to both your physical and spiritual development. Sometimes the energy in a chakra can become blocked by physical injuries, emotional trauma, our beliefs and culture, or even from things that happened in our childhood that have never been addressed. When the chakras are blocked, you may encounter difficulties in your life, but when cleared, life is smoother and more joyous.

When the energy within a chakra becomes stagnant, the chakra needs to be cleared and balanced in order to get the energy flowing correctly again so that you will be grounded and in touch with your physical body and spiritual core essence. Balancing the chakras is a form of energy therapy that will not only bring balance to your chakras but will raise your frequency as well. Chakras can be balanced through yoga, guided meditation, color therapy, aromatherapy, breathing exercises, and meditation, to name a few methods. Once you've found balance in your chakras, you'll experience inner peace and higher levels of confidence and self-esteem as you grow spiritually on your life path.

Finding and Maintaining Balance

When you are working with your intuitive gifts, it is important to find a place of centered balance within your core spiritual self. When you find this balance, you will be better able to see the world around you with clarity and understanding. You'll be happier overall and will find more joy in things that you may have previously ignored.

How do you find balance? First, you must be able to notice when you're out of balance. Think about what causes you worry or fear. Are you anxious, nervous, or completely stressed out? Do you feel overwhelmed and frustrated? Do you feel the need to be in control of everything and everyone around you? If you answered yes to any of these questions, then you're most likely out of balance.

To bring yourself back into balance, you have to look at the way you're thinking, the amount you take on in your life, and how you feel about yourself in mind, body, and spirit. If you discover that you're overly stressed or feeling anxious, then make adjustments in your life to release those things that are causing you to feel overwhelmed. As you do this, you are bringing yourself into balance and will be able to find a true connection to your intuitive gifts. Notice how you feel when you're balanced so that you can come back to this point quickly and efficiently in the future. It's difficult to work with your abilities when you're upset, worried, or anxious. If you let these feelings go, even for a short time, then you'll become balanced, which will have a positive effect on your thinking.

Once you know what this feeling is, to maintain this newfound balance you need only to remember how you felt when you connected to it before and use visualization to quickly get back to this place within you. In your mind's eye, take yourself back to your core essence, the place where you feel at peace, calm, and at one with your true spiritual self. Any time that you feel as though your world is spinning out of control, go back to this place. Remember what it felt like to be centered and balanced; as you reconnect with that part of yourself, you will restore balance within. As you do energy work, or work with your intuitive abilities, it's important always to approach your abilities from a place of centered and balanced oneness so that you're as accurate as possible, especially if you're working with someone else.

Try It Now: An Exercise in Finding Balance

Find a place where you can be alone in complete silence for a few moments. Lie down on your bed, sit in a comfortable chair, or take a shower if it's difficult to find quiet time. Once you're in a quiet environment, imagine that all of the things causing you stress are moving away from you, lightening your load, freeing you from the chaos that the weight of these things causes you. Imagine a big box near your feet where you can store everything for a while. Let your mind and body relax as you're placing a situation into the box. With each one that you add, let yourself relax even more. Is work causing you problems? Put everything associated with work in the box. Maybe you're overwhelmed by your intuition because too much comes in too quickly—put your intuition in the box. Are you dealing with a situation within a personal relationship? Put that issue in the box, too. Once you've placed everything inside, use creative visualization to imagine the lid closing. Now, consider how you're feeling. Do you feel lighter, less worried, and stress-free? Are your mind and body relaxed? If so, you are in your place of balance; you are now "centered." You can return to this place at any time when you need to reconnect to your core essence and regain a feeling of balance. Now, take everything out of the box and examine it as you reclaim it. You'll find that as you look at the situations from a state of balanced centeredness, each one seems less extreme and you may even discover a resolution as you reclaim it.

Meditation/Grounding/Centering

In order to work at your best with your abilities, you have to stay grounded and centered within your own core frequency. If you don't, you'll discover your impressions are often wrong and you feel frazzled, off balance, and easily frustrated. Not only can your psychic abilities be off-kilter, but you will feel out of sync in other areas of your life, too. It can feel as though you've just stuck a metal clothes hanger into a live electrical outlet and you're getting the shock of a lifetime. If you're a medium, you can be overwhelmed by the sheer number of spirits who want to talk to you all at once. In order to be effective as a medium or intuitive, you have to find balance to become more in tune with your intuitive nature.

To bring yourself back into balance, also called "grounding" and "centering," you can use a formal meditation technique or either of the two approaches in the exercise below. I'm giving you both an expanded example and a quick-and-easy version. Both ways are great to use depending on how much time you have to dedicate to it.

_____

Try It Now: Ground and Center Yourself

If you have a lot of time, find a quiet place to sit comfortably with your feet flat on the floor. You can also do the following exercise in a standing position if you prefer.

Using creative visualization, look inside yourself until you find your core essence. The first couple of times you do this, it may be difficult to find, but once you do, you'll always be able to go straight to your core when doing this exercise. Your core is the place inside you that feels like your true self, your soul essence, your spiritual frequency. Once you're connected with your core, imagine white light flowing into you through the top of your head. Let this light flow through you, filling you with love and light. Imagine it reaching out to every cell of your being. As it reaches your feet, allow it to flow into the ground beneath you, grounding you to the earth. As the light fills you, imagine all of your anxiety and frustrations converting to calm peacefulness, centering and balancing your essence. If you're having trouble with the conversion, you can also imagine the light pushing any negativity out of your body through the bottoms of your feet to be absorbed by the earth. Once you feel stable and that you are back in balance, centered, and grounded, close yourself off to the flow of energy and keep all of the light and love inside of you.

There are times when you don't have the time to do a lengthy exercise but instead need a quick fix to balance and center yourself. If you only have a few minutes, then wherever you are, simply close your eyes, take a cleansing breath, and open the crown chakra at the top of your head and let white light fill you. Give the white light the intention to bring you back to a balanced center, and then imagine it filling you in seconds, dissolving any negativity and fulfilling your intention as it does so. Feel your feet planted firmly on the earth, grounding you to it like glue. Close your crown chakra and keep the white light within you. Open your eyes feeling your energy whole and complete instead of frazzled and out of sorts.

Improving Accuracy

As you develop your intuition, you'll notice that it feels different from your normal five senses. The information you receive may come to you in a particular manner. For instance, if your vision always gets a little blurry when you're receiving a clairvoyant impression, it is sign that you are using a sixth sense. Because each of us is a unique individual, the way you receive an impression will be unique to you, although there are some similarities that many people share. With intuition, the more you use it, the more accurate it will become. Practice is a key aspect of becoming more accurate in your impressions.

There are a few things that you should do as you practice using your abilities. Start by just thinking about your gifts. The more you think about them, the more you'll connect to them, even if you're not using them at the time. When you are using your abilities, relax and consciously move to your balanced center. If you're working on receiving clairvoyant impressions, allow those impressions to come to you and believe in them. Don't try to second-guess yourself, because that can cause you to discard the correct impression and listen to your own thoughts and feelings of what you think the impression should be. It is helpful to have someone who will work with you so you can receive impressions for them and they can confirm whether what you're seeing is correct. When you receive feedback from someone, you'll know if you're improving your ability. If you're working alone, practice with events that you can confirm on your own.

Using Your Abilities: Any Place, Any Time

The more you feel at one with your abilities, the easier it will be to use them at any place or at any time. You may start by setting aside a time every day when you can practice enhancing your ability. As time passes, you'll hopefully find that it is easy to quickly receive and interpret impressions accurately. You'll soon find that you don't need to have tools like cards or runes at your disposal, even if you like using them, but will be able to rapidly move from not using your abilities to receiving impressions without doing anything special. This happens because you're growing within your abilities as you move forward on your spiritual path.

Let's compare using your abilities with another example. A professional sprinter practices on the track, making his body toned and muscular. During competitions, he runs based on his training, body strength, and dexterity. But what happens off the track? Let's say he sees a child about to step out into traffic. Using his training and ability to run fast, he's able to get to the child quickly and save his life. This athlete is able to use his abilities any place and any time other than what he specifically trained for because the sprinting skill has become a part of him. Your intuitive abilities are a part of you as well. Once you've become accustomed to using your abilities, you can use them at any place and any time, just like the athlete. You will not need to sit at a special place or have specific things around you to receive impressions when you're away from your working area and tools. The impressions will come to you through your "clair" abilities whenever you need them (see chapter three).

Honor Your Gifts

Being intuitive is a gift that you have received in order to obtain a glimpse into the past, present, or future. Honor this gift by being true to yourself, honest in your impressions, and sincere in your desire to do good deeds on the earthly plane when using your gifts.

By honoring these gifts as part of your inner knowledge and soul truth, you are embracing all of your spiritual essence. When you honor your intuition by using it for the greater good, you are allowing yourself to accept all that you are, which can help you overcome any issues or situations that you may be experiencing in your life.

Learn to honor and respect your intuitive gifts through use. Ask questions and receive the response without allowing your rational, logical, thinking mind to get in the way. Believe in the impressions you receive, the words you hear, or the vision you see as a personal truth or a message that will help someone else embrace their own truth. You have been given your gifts for a reason; use them to enhance and embrace your true soul essence as you make your way on the earthly plane.

The Power in Secrets

If someone told you a secret, would you share it? Are you a person who keeps your mouth shut when a secret is told to you, or does it eat away at you until you just have to tell someone else? Not only does keeping secrets make you a person of honor and integrity, but it also gives you power. This isn't power over the person who told you the secret, but a Universal strength of soul. When you keep the secrets of others, you are defined as a trustworthy and reliable person.

What if the secret is your own? Do you tell others? Sometimes it's better to keep your secrets to yourself, because by holding them tightly to you, you'll inevitably give them more power, more of a chance to grow and become all that they are supposed to be in your life. Some secrets, when shared, lose strength and can even go away. Let's look at an example. Let's say you've come up with an idea for a new product, something that hasn't ever been done before. You've keep this secret to yourself for a long time, building it up in your mind, considering how you can make it work and offer it to the public. Then one day you're having lunch with your best friend, whom you haven't told your secret, and suddenly you feel like you should tell. So you do. A few months later, you see your product available on television. Did someone overhear what you said in the restaurant or did they also receive this idea from the Universe? You may never know for sure, but in this situation, by telling the idea you took away its power. Keeping a secret to maintain its power can be a positive action. There are also times when telling a secret that is causing harm can give you a boost in frequency. For example, if a person is being abused and is afraid to tell, then releasing the secret by telling someone they trust frees them from the negative holds of that secret and allows them to take the appropriate measures to stop the abuse.

....

Now that you've learned some of the ways that your intuition can help you achieve positive spiritual growth, it's time to put those abilities to use. Take your time and consider all of the factors regarding the use of your abilities and how they are bringing about spiritual enlightenment for you. As you move along this path, you will also discover things that are unique to you that will bring about growth and understanding. Keep your eyes and mind open as you undertake this journey.

Two

Tools to Use in Developing Your Abilities

There are many tools that you can use while you are developing your intuition. Some of these tools you will always use, while others you will discard as you move past needing them to achieve your goals. In this chapter, you'll learn about some of these tools and how they can work for you. Try each of them. If they feel right to you, embrace them as your own; if they don't, discard them for the time being. When and if the time is right, you'll come back to them and try again.

White Light of Divinity Protection

White light protection can be used in many ways to remove negative energy from your person and environment. Once the negativity is removed, white light is also used to protect you from any new negative energy that could cause you problems. White light is the purest, divine energy, which we're allowed to use for our own protection and to protect those we love. You can use the White Light of Divinity to cleanse your home or to help you in certain situations such as clearing phone lines. Some people use specific prayers and methods when using white light, and this is fine if you have the time for a ritual, but I never do. I believe that spiritually we are allowed to use the White Light of Divinity as needed, so I thank the Universe each time I use it. I don't make a big ordeal out of it because I'm always busy; the easier it is for me to do an exercise, the better.

Using white light is extremely easy and quick to do. To use white light as protection, you are going to use creative visualization to imagine white light flowing from the Universe to you. Imagine it as a brilliantly glowing, bright, pure light of energy forming a bubble around you, starting above your head, and moving down until it goes underneath the ground at your feet. Now you're completely enclosed in this protective light. For more protection, you can add several layers of light and give the bubble different dimensions by making it closer or farther away from you. When you're putting the layers of light around you, focus on its brilliance, purity, and positivity. Watch as it creates a barrier around you that doesn't allow any negative energy to cross. You can also use creative visualization to put mirrors on the outside of the white light so that any negativity sent your way reflects back to its source.

You can use White Light of Divinity to protect yourself, loved ones, your property, and your pets by using the same method described above. If you have fears, use it to help eliminate those fears. For example, if you're afraid of driving on the interstate, the next time you have to take that route, put several layers of white light around you before you get on the interstate. Make sure it goes underneath the tires and that you give the light the intention of moving with your vehicle. Also put it around yourself inside the vehicle. White light protection can be used at any time you need it. Use it often.

Psychic Tests

I want to start this section by saying that if you're going to do psychic tests, try to avoid the ones online. These are electronic guessing games and aren't a true gauge of your real ability. If you're doing them just for fun, that's one thing, but if you're trying to accurately determine your level of ability, they don't work.

Written tests that ask you about your experiences are better indicators of your abilities. When you're answering questions based on your real life experiences, you know for sure whether or not you've had that experience or the types of tendencies you're being asked about and can give an accurate, honest answer and obtain a result. If you're intuitive, you already know it on a deep soul level. Parapsychology is the study of psychic abilities in real-world settings; these types of tests will be more accurate. If you truly want to be tested, you can contact a legitimate department of parapsychology.

The best way I've found to analyze your intuitive abilities is to test yourself. You can practice increasing the strength of your abilities by using and assessing them based on this usage. Try this: Think of a friend and send them an energy thought that they should contact you at a specific time during the day. If that person calls or shows up at that time, then your abilities worked. Psychic abilities are difficult to test, but when you have things happen to you repeatedly, then there's no doubt that you have them. Believe in yourself and your abilities.

Talisman/Amulet

A talisman or amulet is often a sign to others that the wearer has a belief in metaphysical principles and probably possesses intuitive abilities. Many intuitives like to wear a talisman or amulet either as a necklace or bracelet; some choose to carry it on their person out of public view. There are differences between an amulet and a talisman, but you'll use the same programming when you make them. I've found that it's much better to create your own talisman or amulet than to have someone else make one for you. When you design it yourself, you're using your soul energy, frequency, and intuition to give the talisman or amulet a specific intention that is unique to your spiritual being. If you bought the item you're using, all future energy associated with it is yours once you clear it of any energy that it may have absorbed prior to your purchase.

An amulet is used for protection from negative energy of any kind, whether it's coming from the physical plane or from low-level entities on the spiritual plane. Amulets protect you from any kind of hostility, pessimism, or negative intent from the human, spirit, and animal worlds.

A talisman is used to attract specifically desired results such as increasing psychic abilities, spiritual insights, career success, greater positivity in your life, wisdom, knowledge, strength, or courage. Many people who work with the law of attraction also use a talisman programmed for what they want to attract into their life. Talismans are powerful tools. You can use them to aid in manifesting things in your life or to help you reach certain goals—basically for any purpose you need. You can also "double program" a talisman so that it attracts your intended purpose and provides protection. When you charge the item, you should choose whether it will act actively as a talisman and passively as an amulet or vice versa. For example, you may passively charge a pendant that you'll wear around your neck as a talisman to protect you from negative energies you encounter and actively charge a coin that you tuck inside your purse or wallet to attract more money to you.

When creating an amulet or talisman, you'll first choose an object that you like. It may or may not contain a stone or crystal, but if it does, the energy of that stone or crystal will enhance it. Once you've selected your item, hold it between your hands and envision white light cleansing it, washing away any energy from people who may have touched the item prior to your purchasing it. Now, give the item purpose. Send a telepathic message to the item stating that it will be used for the specific purpose you have in mind. Then give your energy to the item, connecting it to you. Whenever you wear or carry the item, think of its purpose as you handle it or wear it. You may feel heat from the item as it works on your behalf. You can make different ones that have different intentions and wear them all together or separately as needed.

Pendulum

A pendulum is a divination tool that is used to obtain answers to questions. In its basic form, it is a weight on a string. Many people make their own pendulums by tying a piece of thread to a ring or using a threaded needle. Other pendulums are made out of stones or crystals secured to a chain and the presentation can be plain or ornate. Some pendulums can be easily converted to a necklace so that it can be worn when not in use. You can buy beautiful boxes, bags, or cases to store your pendulum if you're not wearing or using it.

Pendulums are often used to answer yes or no questions or to provide insights into your own truth and inner wisdom through connection to your higher self and your subconscious mind. You've probably heard that every answer is within you. A pendulum can help you uncover those answers to the questions you have about yourself, life, the Universe, or future events. The most popular use of a pendulum is to obtain answers to questions by connecting to your higher self, your soul essence, or by asking your guides to use the pendulum with you as a tool of enlightenment. It is also used to monitor your being on a soul level by helping in developing your intuition, balancing chakras, increasing your frequency, balancing your aura, and determining whether a spirit is around you. Most pendulums are used to help find answers you may need on a daily basis, but they are also used in dowsing to find water, minerals, and other items under the ground or to find lost objects.

To use a pendulum, either one that you've made or purchased, you will first clear your mind and fill yourself with positive energy while imagining a bubble of white protective light around you. Hold your pendulum by the end of the string or chain, or hold the middle of the chain if you feel you should; just don't hold it too close to the actual pendulum. You want to make sure you have enough string or chain to get free-flowing movement. Many people hold the pendulum over the palm of their hand during a session but you can also hold it over a table, book, or any other surface. When asking about pregnancy, it is often held over the woman's abdomen. Whatever surface you use, you'll touch the tip of the pendulum to the surface between questions to indicate that the question has been answered.

Next, set the motions that will be answers. You can do this by telling the pendulum which movement goes with which action or by asking "What motion means yes? What motion means no?" and so on; after each question, watch the direction the pendulum moves in response. The most common choices are an up and down movement for "yes"; a side to side motion for "no"; a clockwise circle for "maybe"; and a counterclockwise motion for "I don't know," "I can't," or "I don't want to say." Do a couple of test questions to make sure everything is working right. If I use a pendulum, I always set where the answers are coming from—my subconscious mind, my higher self, or my spirit guides—so that I know I'm not moving the pendulum myself for an answer that I prefer. At this time, you'll begin asking questions. If the pendulum doesn't move, you will probably need to rephrase the question. Don't rush it. Give the pendulum time to move before you start rephrasing questions too quickly.

You'll notice that sometimes the pendulum will swing very strongly and at other times gently. The stronger the movement, the more adamant the response you've received. When you've finished your session with the pendulum, clear the energy from the session before putting it away.

Manifestation/Manifestation Board

Manifestation at its root is thought. Manifestation is when you're using creative visualization while practicing the law of attraction to materialize what you want in your life. The law of attraction is a metaphysical belief that like attracts like; in other words, positive thinking brings about positive physical results and negative thinking brings about negative physical results. According to the law of attraction, it's all in the phrasing. If you say, "I need more money," you will continue to "need more money." If you rephrase this while focusing your thoughts on the end goal of having more money instead of the problem of needing more money, then you might say, "I will have more money," thereby bringing more money into your life.

When you practice manifestation, you are placing a positive intention on your needs, desires, and goals, and holding that thought until what you desire appears in your life. You are adjusting your personal vibration to positively attract what you desire into your life by using energy to align yourself with it. If your intention is strong and clear, then the object will appear sooner rather than later. If your intention is weak and unfocused, it will take longer. During manifestation, start out with clear, concise goals.

Make a manifestation board to aid in bringing your desires to you. The manifestation board is your own personal collage of the things that you need or want in your life, and is used as you practice the law of attraction to manifest these things. When you create a physical expression of these needs and desires in the form of a board, you're telling the Universe that you're ready to receive these new things, feelings, or events in your life. When you create the board, center yourself before you begin and then make the board with focus and intention. The energy that you continually put into the board through feelings, thoughts, desires, and intentions brings the objects on your board closer to you. It's giving creative visualization a physical place to reside (on the board).

Now that you have decided what you need and want, the next thing is to cut pictures out of magazines that represent these things and glue them on the board. The board can be made of poster board, cardboard, or paper. Arrange the photos so that the most important thing is on top and the remaining items in the order you desire them, or you can place them in whatever shape or pattern you feel moved to place them. You can also cut out words and glue them on the board or write in words that verbalize what you want to manifest in positive terms. Once you've finished creating the board, place it on the wall or somewhere you will see it often and release your energy ties to it. This means that you will release each item on the board and hand it over to the Universe to bring into your life. When it appears, write "thank you" under the item and the date that it manifested so that you recognize its appearance in your life.

Mirrors

You've heard the children's dares. Maybe you've even done them. You go into the bathroom, lock the door, turn off the light, and say "Bloody Mary" three times while turning in a circle. When you look into the mirror, Bloody Mary will be there, covered in blood that drips from her knife. Isn't that a lovely way to scare a child half to death? Mirrors have always been an object of fascination when it comes to the spirit world. They are said to reflect the image of a spirit, act as a portal, and do a variety of other things (some of which aren't necessarily true).

I know for a fact that spirits can manifest in mirrors because I've seen spirits through them. Once I'd been blow-drying my hair (which was very long at the time), so I'd bent over a bit so I could get to the back better. When I stood up, I saw the reflection of a blond-haired girl about ten years old standing in the bathroom doorway and heard the words, "It will be okay, but be prepared for change." I immediately looked at the door but there wasn't anyone there. I went to check on my kids in their room, and they hadn't invited anyone over. The girl just vanished. But she was right. Within several weeks everything changed and our lives were turned upside down. It all worked out okay, just as she'd said. I've since learned that her name is Ally and she's one of my guides.

Try It Now:
Connect with Your Spiritual Nature through a Mirror

You can use a mirror to intuitively connect to your soul. In doing this exercise, you can determine what your abilities are and the best way for you to use them because you're tuning in to your true essence. What you'll do is use a mirror that doesn't have a sink in front of it—you'll want to be able to stand close to the mirror instead of leaning toward it. Pick out your mirror, protect yourself with white light, stand there and stare into your own eyes. Let your mind clear, find your center, and ground yourself to the earth. Now spread the fingers of your right hand wide. One at a time, place your fingertips on the mirror. As each fingertip connects, imagine it opening a portal that connects you to the Other Side, to your true spiritual essence, and give each fingertip an intention. Your intention may be something like, "Show me the best way to understand my empathic ability," "I want to see the path I mapped out for myself," or maybe, "I am afraid of my abilities; show me how to erase this fear." If you only want to work on one thing at a time, repeat the same intention as you place each fingertip on the mirror. Now, intuitively look past your physical eyes and into your soul essence. It may take a few minutes to connect, but once you do, you are within yourself at the purest and most basic level. Listen to messages from your higher self and any guides that show up to help you.

....

As you move along your path, there will be additional tools that will be of use to you if you need them. As they come into your life, give them a fair chance of helping you to achieve further enlightenment. You may only need them for a short time; then again, you may feel such an affinity to them that you continue to use them as you grow and develop your intuitive abilities throughout your lifetime. Tools are there to assist you. Use them as you see fit.

Three

Discovering Your "Clair" Abilities

The "clair" abilities are the bare bones of intuitive development. Everyone has them and they can be strong or weak depending upon where you are in your spiritual growth. You can develop each of your clair abilities and make them stronger. Let's take a look at each of them and how you can make them work for you.

Clairvoyance/Clairvoyant

Clairvoyance is a French and Latin word that means "clear vision"—the intuitive ability to see visions without using your eyes, an intuitive knowledge of people and things, to perceive within the mind's eye (the third eye, which is located in the middle of the forehead) something that exists on the spiritual or ethereal realm. A clairvoyant is the person who is able to obtain information about past, present, and future events from other dimensions using the third eye and not the physical eyes. They can see what normally cannot be seen physically. If you are clairvoyant, you may see spirits, auras, angels, guides, and others. You may also see scenes that explain situations in others' lives. Clairvoyance is the process of obtaining this information. For those who have the gift of clairvoyance, you can see past the veil to the spiritual realms and receive messages from departed loved ones or obtain information from a higher source, such as spirit guides. If you're also clairaudient, you may hear these guides and loved ones speak to you, but we'll get to that in a minute.

Clairvoyance can manifest in different ways. You may see an entire scene play out like a movie running through your head; you may see words, numbers, or objects that give you an overall intuitive impression; or you may see the physical manifestation of your guide or another entity delivering a message. When my abilities first started developing, I knew when I would have a clairvoyant vision because my physical vision would change. Whatever was in front of me would disappear and I saw what looked like a television channel that had gone off the air. All that was on the screen was the black-and-white snow, then that would fade and I'd see a scene playing out like a movie. When it was over, my vision would go back to that snowy screen, then that would disappear and I would be able to see regularly again. Once I was able to recognize a clairvoyant vision for what it was, the snowy screen before and after the vision stopped happening.

Clairvoyance feels like the information is coming from outside of you. You may be watching a scene unfold in your mind's eye, but the information itself isn't part of your being. It feels as if it's outside of your physical and emotional self, just as you'd feel if you were seeing a movie in a theater. It's something that you watch instead of experiencing it as your own internal thought process or emotion. As you discover more about your clairvoyant nature, look for signs that what you're picking up is coming from outside of you instead of coming from within you. Do you see a snowy screen like I did? Or maybe you always see visions of events that have happened in the past on your left side and future events always seem to happen on your right side. This is a clue that what you're experiencing is clairvoyant in nature.

The importance of clairvoyance is that you recognize you are seeing an event happen, whether it's in the past, present, or future. You might be able to connect your clairvoyant experiences with reality, confirming your abilities are on track. You may also recognize it as something that hasn't happened yet. The important thing with a clairvoyant experience is that you use the information to help yourself or others.

Clairaudience/Clairaudient

Clairaudience means "clear hearing," and is the ability to hear sounds from the spiritual world that are inaudible to others. It is intuitively hearing that which isn't audible from a physical source but instead originates from the spiritual realm. This may include music, voices, and ordinary sounds such as doors closing, keys jiggling, or someone making noise as they move around the house in daily activity when you know that there isn't anyone on the physical plane that could be making the noise.

Sometimes these sounds can be loud and quite noticeable, while at other times they are merely a whisper. Clairaudient intuitives can often hear spirits speak to them just as clearly as they can hear you talk. They may hear music, knocking, or other sounds without a physical source, or pick up entire conversations when no one else is around. Any sound coming from the spiritual realm (the Other Side) that you can hear but your best friend standing right beside you cannot hear is clairaudient in nature.

Most often, clairaudient sounds are associated with spirit guides, angels, or deceased loved ones speaking to you in order to deliver messages, but sometimes they are just random noises. They can be related to the paranormal, which is why clairaudient intuitives can often pick up specific messages in places thought to be haunted. You may also tap in to a portal (a place spiritual beings use to travel between the realms of existence). If this is the case, you can usually pinpoint the portal to one specific location by listening to where the sounds originate.

So what does it feel like to be clairaudient? Have you heard someone shout your name when no one was around? If a clairaudient intuitive is distracted or not paying attention when someone from the spiritual realm is trying to deliver a message, they will sometimes shout just to get your attention, especially if it's an important message. If you hear your name being shouted, take a few moments and focus your intuitive abilities in order to hear the message. Sometimes you'll get it immediately and other times it may be hours later, but the shouting of your name increases your awareness so that when the message comes, you're open to receive it. This type of clairaudience feels as if you're hearing it with your normal hearing. Other clairaudient sounds feel like they're in your head or coming from a specific place outside of yourself, such as the corner of a room.

When I do readings and spirit guides come with messages for the person I'm doing a reading for, I hear them talk in my mind and I normally just type what I'm hearing so that the message is as accurate as possible. Other times, I'll hear the message as if someone is standing beside me talking. If you're developing your abilities, make sure you're paying attention to the sounds around you. Ask others if they hear what you're hearing; soon, you'll be able to recognize what is coming from the spiritual realm and is truly clairaudient.

Clairscent/Clairscentrist

Clairscent is the ability to smell something clearly that does not have an origin on our physical level of existence but originates from the spirit realm. A clairscentrist is an intuitive who can smell these scents or odors and who can interpret the meaning of a smell and whether there is a message being delivered with the scent.

The most important factor in knowing that you are a clairscentrist is whether or not you are able to find physical causes for the aromas that you smell. You have to look high and low to rule out even remote possibilities before attributing the scent to the spiritual realm. You don't want the smell of a rotting potato in your pantry to make you think that spirit is trying to deliver a message associated with someone who disliked potatoes—chances are, there's a bad potato hiding in the bag you purchased last week. If you live in an apartment building, condo, duplex, or other type of attached building, you have to make sure that the scents aren't somehow coming into your home from someone else's residence. If they aren't, then the scent is probably originating from the spiritual realm and you have to use your intuitive abilities to determine why you smell the particular fragrance. Another good indication that the scent is otherworldly in nature is if you're the only one that smells it. When you have a clairscent experience around others, you can determine the root of the smell more quickly than if you're alone because you're able to ask other people if they smell the same thing.

Scents, aromas, and even pungent odors come to intuitives for specific reasons. For instance, say that a relative has passed over but has a message that he or she wants to deliver to someone left behind. Then the scent associated with the person may be apparent to the intuitive. There have been numerous times that I've smelled specific perfumes during a reading or other things like cigar smoke, cigarette smoke, pipes, mothballs, rain, specific foods cooking, and so on. The reason for these smells was specifically to help confirm the identity of the spirit visiting.

Your guides can also send you messages using scent. Let's say you have a hard time staying emotionally calm in times of stress but the smell of lilacs always seems to calm you. Then one day you're at work—everything is going wrong and you're at your wits end. Suddenly, you are overwhelmed with the scent of lilacs. You immediately begin to calm down and try to find the source of the smell, but can't. In this situation, your guides have stepped in to give you a little reprieve during a stressful time.

Oftentimes scents that are picked up by a clairscentrist will be very strong, but they can also be very fleeting and light. If you're tuned into your intuitive abilities you will register both, regardless of the strength of the impression.

Clairempathy/Clairempathic

Clairempathy means "clear emotion," or to feel the emotions and attitudes of another within one's self. It is feeling another person's emotions, mental thoughts, and physical energy without prior knowledge of how that person feels. This is what an empath experiences. Sometimes these feelings can be overwhelming, especially if a large group of people is involved in some tragedy. Being an empath can be very draining unless you learn to filter the emotions and keep them distant and separate from your own inner energy.

As a clairempathic, you may also understand a person's true inner feelings even if they are able to hide them on the outside. Sometimes it can be very difficult to separate your own feelings from empathic feelings originating from another person. As an empath, you should learn to recognize when the feelings are coming from outside of your being and be aware that they are not your emotions at all.

I've always believed that clairempathy is one of the hardest intuitive abilities to control. Sometimes you're just hit broadside with overwhelming feelings that seem to come out of nowhere. You find yourself crying or are jubilantly happy without reason. Usually the reasons are revealed later, when you recognize that it was your empathic abilities causing the feelings and not your own experiences.

Here's a situation that I experienced that shows empathic abilities in action. Recently, I had a week of crying jags where I'd get an overwhelming feeling of sadness and just burst into tears. It actually got to the point that it was annoying me. At first I thought I was just being overly emotional; as more time went by, it just didn't make sense that I'd burst into tears for no apparent reason. Toward the end of the week, I was talking with an intuitive friend only to discover that she'd had the same thing happen to her within the same time period. Incidentally, my crying jags took place right after a series of tornadoes devastated the Midwest and the Mississippi flooded to the extreme. While I knew what was going on in the world, I don't watch the news regularly because I'm empathic and it can sometimes be very overwhelming for me. I hadn't realized that what I felt was a result of the sadness in the Midwest until my friend pointed out the connection. Sometimes you have to remember to check your feelings to make sure they're your own. In this situation, I hadn't done that. As soon as I checked my feelings, I realized that the emotions were indeed coming from outside of me, and the feelings stopped just as suddenly as they'd begun.

Try It Now: Clairempathy

For this exercise, turn on the television and watch the news. You may have to switch channels until you find a news report that you feel drawn to. As you watch the report, pay particular attention to the emotions you're feeling. Are they coming from outside of you? Or are they your emotions? If they are coming from outside of you, you're probably connecting empathically with the people in the report. Notice and write down how you feel and any impressions that you receive. Over the next few days, follow the report to see if any of your impressions happened or if you can confirm that you picked up on the feelings of someone involved in the story, which will often be revealed through further news reports.

Clairgustance/Clairgustant

Clairgustance is the ability to experience taste from the spiritual realm that is associated with a specific person, place, or thing without putting anything in your mouth. This ability can be connected to the present, past, or future. An intuitive who has this ability is a clairgustant. Clairgustance is also referred to as "clairsavorance" and a clairgustant as a "clairsavorant." Both terms are used interchangeable to refer to the ability of "clear tasting" and the intuitive who has the ability.

Clairgustance is often experienced when in the alpha state of consciousness (when you're meditating or daydreaming), but can also come on suddenly and for no apparent reason when you're fully conscious and far from the alpha state of mind. It often accompanies other abilities such as clairvoyance or clairscent.

If you've ever had a sudden, strange taste in your mouth and you couldn't figure out where it was coming from, then you may have unknowingly experienced clairgustance. Let me give you a few fictional examples of how this ability might present itself in your life. Once you understand how it works then you'll be more aware if you experience it. Let's pretend you are a nurse and one day at work an elderly lady comes in for a yearly visit. While you're taking her blood pressure, you suddenly taste oranges. The feeling persists until the woman leaves. When her blood work comes back several days later, you notice that she was very low in vitamin C. Coincidence? No. You were given an impression through taste. The next time, though, you'll be more likely to recognize what is happening. Now let's pretend you're a police officer who is dealing with a crime. You have a distinct taste of antifreeze in your mouth; even though you don't know what antifreeze tastes like, you sense that it is antifreeze as you experience this taste. When the crime is solved, antifreeze was indeed a component. Or maybe your experience is one that has nothing to do with work. Maybe you're sitting at home one night watching something on the television when you're suddenly tasting your grandmother's biscuits covered in butter and gravy. It is her favorite recipe and she makes them for you every time you visit. Moments later the phone rings and it's your grandmother. This taste is letting you know that your grandmother was about to call or that she was thinking about you.

While there isn't really a way to practice this ability, if you are aware that it exists, you may begin to notice times when taste accompanies other intuitive information that you may receive. Once aware, you can obtain a well-rounded overall impression including taste.

Clairsentience/Clairsentient

Clairsentience is a feeling that comes out of the blue that you feel in your whole body, oftentimes specifically in the pit of your stomach. The intuitive who experiences this ability is a clairsentient. Because this ability tends to settle in the stomach area, it's often called a "gut feeling." In this instance, the intuitive has an insight or "knowing" of a hidden or forgotten fact. They feel it throughout their whole body without any outside stimulation. For instance, you may know the phone is going to ring before it does, or you think of someone and they show up on your doorstep or you run into them at the store. This is the ability to attain direct knowledge or cognition without rational thought or inference. If you have this ability, you may also feel those in the spirit realm.

Everyone has clairsentience even if you think you don't have any abilities at all. It's important in your development to pay close attention to these clear feelings because it is through them that you will gain greater insight into all of your abilities.

If you've ever felt suddenly uncomfortable as though you were being watched, then discovered someone staring at you, that's clairsentience. Clairsentience also warns you of danger, potentially negative outcomes, or situations that should be avoided. Maybe you were at a job interview and got a sinking feeling in the pit of your stomach; even though there were no obvious reasons behind your feelings, you declined the job when it was offered to you because of those feelings. Several months later, you discovered the person who interviewed you was embezzling money from the company and was using the person in the position you applied for as a cover for their activities. Had you not listened to your clairsentience, you would not have avoided that negative situation.

Another way this ability manifests is in first impressions. When you meet someone for the first time, you may have a light, airy feeling, tingling sensations, a sinking feeling in your stomach, or feel pressure throughout your body. Depending on the nature of how you're feeling, you may either intensely like or dislike the person. Usually this sensation isn't wrong, but it's often hindsight that shows you clearly why you felt the way you did during your first meeting. Take a moment right now and think back on some of the people you've known and how you felt when you first met them. Was your initial feeling correct?

Clairsentience during first impressions doesn't always apply to people. It can also occur with situations that you may be involved in. It's always a good idea to listen to the intuitive pushes and pulls within your body and the sensations you're feeling during first impressions. Once you listen, you need to take the action that you feel to be correct at the time.

Contact with spirit, whether it's a guide or other entity, will bring forth your clairsentient abilities. You may feel cold chills or the sensation that the hair on the back of your neck is standing up. You may feel as if you're being watched but when you turn, no one is there. Most mediums are clairsentient.

As you research intuitive abilities, you will probably find clairsentience grouped together with clairtangency (psychometry) and clairempathy, but I consider these to be three distinct abilities. While they all work together, each is unique and presents itself differently. While you're learning to understand your abilities, you will make greater progress by sorting out your individual talents and then learning how they all work together as a whole.

Clairtangency/Psychometry

Clairtangency means "clear touching," the ability to touch beyond the physical, and is commonly referred to as psychometry. It is using your intuitive sense of touch to interpret the energy contained within an object and obtain knowledge that wasn't previously known. You can receive information about the object's history and the people who owned or touched it in the past or present. Psychometry is an interesting ability to have because it allows you to learn the history of an object and the people connected to it.

While psychometry is usually associated with physical inanimate objects, you can also receive impressions when touching another person. Have you brushed up against someone you didn't know and suddenly sensed something about that person through feelings or a vision? That's psychometry at work. Had you not come into physical contact with the person, you probably wouldn't have received the impression. Psychometry often works in conjunction with your other psychic abilities. In this example, touching the person led to a clairempathic or clairvoyant impression.

Try It Now: Psychometry

A good way to practice psychometry is to visit a department store and make a conscious effort to pick up information about the people who have come into contact with an object before you. Choose a shirt. Hold it, feel the fabric, maybe even take it to a dressing room and try it on. Can you pick up impressions about someone who tried the shirt on before you or the employee who unpacked it and hung it on the rack? You may go back further to the shipper or the manufacturer or even the person who made the fabric. Let your mind be open to whatever impressions you receive. Once you've tried this activity, move on to one where you can prove whether what you're seeing is right or wrong.

This time, you're going to visit an antique store. Most employees in antique stores will know something of the history of the item because that history is what helps to sell it. If you visit an antique shop where the employee is clueless about the history of the merchandise, try another one until you find a knowledgeable staff. When you visit, take your time walking through the store. Touch the merchandise, especially if there are large pieces of wood furniture, which often hold on to previous energies associated with them, to see what kind of impressions you receive. If you find yourself drawn to one particular piece, touch it until you have a clear vision of its history and then verify that history with the employee. The more you practice this, the better you will become. It's also instant validation as to whether you're right or wrong in your impressions if the employee can give you the history of the object. You can also do this with pictures of people you don't know or objects that belong to people you don't know. For example, have a friend get an object from someone they know (who you don't know) and try the same exercise.

Claircognizance/Claircognizant

If you've known something to be true without knowing how you knew it, you've tapped into your claircognizant ability. Claircognizance means "clear knowing," or anomalous cognition. The information comes to you suddenly and you just know without a doubt that the information is truth, even if you're not qualified to know and don't know how you know. An example of a claircognizant is someone who doesn't know anything about gardening, but upon seeing a garden, knows the exact reason the corn isn't growing to its full height and suggests a different combination of fertilizer and water to correct the problem. Or, they may simply say, "It isn't planted deep enough." It's a sure answer expressed as fact without a hint of doubt surrounding the statement. The person "just knows" what is wrong with the corn.

Claircognizant information is given to us from our higher selves or from the spiritual realm. To us, it seems to come out of the blue, without a source or reason for knowing the information. Because of this, it may be hard to convince another person that what you suddenly know is truth, even though you feel it deep in your soul. Let's revisit that job interview I mentioned earlier. What if, right in the middle of the interview, you knew that if you took the job it would ruin your life? You knew this as fact even though there wasn't any reason at this point in time to feel this way, and declined the offer that would have led you to work for a boss who was arrested for embezzlement. Because you acted on this claircognizant information, you protected yourself.

Everyone has some degree of claircognizant ability. It can let you know when someone is lying to you, when you're on the right path, or when it's time to change direction. Claircognizant information will pop in at random times, when you're thinking about something entirely different from the claircognizant information you receive. Just be careful of the manner in which you deliver the information so that you're not perceived as a know-it-all because you're so sure in your claircognizant knowledge.

You can tell the difference between your claircognizant thoughts and normal thoughts because there is no fear attached to the claircognizant information. With a regular thought, you may worry that you're wrong; with a claircognizant thought, there is no doubt in your mind that you're right. You may be asked, "How do you know?" and the only way you can respond is, "I just know." The thought will also feel very clear to you. The energy will be strong and sure. It may come to you when you're doing mundane tasks, when you're in the middle of a conversation, or when you're focusing on work. However it comes, it will probably be out of the blue, and if you feel it in the depths of your soul as truth without the association of fear, that's a sure sign that it's your claircognizant ability.

....

Did you recognize your clair abilities in the above descriptions? Maybe you even connected with an ability that you weren't sure you had but now makes perfect sense to you. As you continue on this path, use your abilities so that they become stronger and aid you when you need them. You may even discover that they are so intricately woven into your being that using them will become part of your daily routine.

Four

✦

Subtle Signs
of Intuition

✦

As we go about our day, our intuition is right there with us, helping us along, showing us signs, and giving us insights to the situations we find ourselves involved in at work and at home. In this chapter, you'll discover some of the subtle ways your intuition presents itself and how you can use it. Try the exercises as you read this chapter. They will help to enhance your intuition.

The Telephone

How is the telephone a sign of intuitive ability? When we use the telephone, our energy connects to the energy of the other person on the line.

If you're in tune with your intuition when you place a call and you get an answering machine or voicemail, you may also pick up impressions about the person you've called. You might sense that they're at the store, or getting a haircut, or working in their flower garden. So you leave a message and wait for them to call you back. Because of your ability to connect to another person's energy, you may sense that they are going to call moments before the phone rings. Or you will know who is calling as soon as you hear the phone ringing.

One of the best ways to practice your psychic abilities, specifically clairvoyance, is to use this psychic connection to other people when using the telephone. I'm going to give you a few exercises that you can try. The more you do these, the more accurate you will become in your intuitive impressions.

Try It Now:
Connect with the Energy of the Telephone

The first exercise you can do is to think of someone whom you would like to talk to on the phone. Imagine your energy connecting to them and intuitively send them a request to call you sometime during the day. This does two things. It increases your psychic awareness because, as you wait for the call, you'll send out positive energy to that person each time you think of them calling you. Then when the phone does ring, you can use your abilities to determine if the person you've sent the request to is the one calling. Don't choose more than one person at a time, though, because then it can turn into a guessing game instead of focused practice in using your ability. When the person calls, validating your energy connection, you've confirmed that your impression was correct.

The second exercise is more random and only applies to incoming calls. In this exercise, you're going to use your psychic ability to determine who is calling when the phone rings. When the phone rings for the first time, focus on connecting to the energy of the person calling. Do you sense that it's a family member, friend, or telemarketer? If it's a friend or family member, can you tell whom? Make a clear decision based on what you sense in the energy field and then answer the phone. Were you right? If not, keep practicing and soon you'll discover that you're correct in knowing who is calling more often than you're wrong.

Thinking of People

One of the ways your abilities work is when you're thinking of another person and that person either shows up, calls you, or connects through social media. Usually these events will be quite random and other times, you just know that you're going to connect with the person you've had on your mind.

Usually the person who comes to mind is someone that you haven't had contact with in a while. You may think of them out of the blue, wonder what they are up to, and, just like a song getting stuck in your head, you can't seem to stop thinking about them. Other times, you'll have a fleeting thought of the person and then forget about them. Then later in the day, you'll either run into them in a public place or you'll connect with them in some other manner. The feeling can also be so strong that you seek the person out. When the two of you do connect, you might realize that you were thinking about each other at the same time.

In these situations, your energy is connecting with their energy. When you think of someone, you're sending out energy into the Universe to that person, and vice versa, which may inspire either of you to connect with the other. The same thing happens when you think of someone and then randomly run into that person in a store or in an online social media setting. The energy connects and you are drawn to each other's energy. This subtle sign of your psychic abilities at work usually has a reason behind it. You may not see the reason at the time but in your spiritual path, there is one. It may be that the person you encounter needs something from you or you may need something from them, even if that something is just a recommendation to connect to a third party. It could also be to forgive a past wrong or clear up a misunderstanding. Whatever the reason behind the encounter, it may be immediately apparent, it may become more apparent as the two of you reconnect, or it might not be clear until hindsight.

Let me give you an example that happens to me quite often. I'm a talker so when I get an impression of someone like this, and I know how to contact the person by phone, I'll call and say, "What's up?" This is usually met with laughter and the response that they were just thinking of calling me to ask me something about intuitive abilities or they need a reading. This ability can also be used with purpose by shouting out the person's name telepathically or with your voice into the Universal Energy and asking them to call you. That kind of purpose associated with intuitive energy usually gets the message delivered and a timely return call.

Sensing Things That Others Can't

When you have intuitive abilities, there are many times that you will pick up on information that others around you (who may or may not be as in tune with their intuitive nature) will not sense. Depending upon the type of abilities that you have, you may also feel or see spirits, pick up on other's thoughts, or get a vision about someone. You may find yourself in some awkward situations because you may not want to know the information you just received.

This happens because you're in tune with your abilities. You are connecting to the energies within the world and the energy of the people around you. As your abilities grow and develop, you'll find that you'll receive more information even when you're not trying. The littlest thing can set it off. You may meet someone for the first time, shake their hand, and see personal information about that person—sometimes information that they do not want known. You didn't ask for the information;

you just saw it in a flash of vision, felt it empathically, or suddenly knew something about the person.

Say you're shopping with a friend and you're the only shoppers in the store. You're browsing near the back when an old lady walks in, says her name is Susan, and strikes up a conversation with you. Your friend thinks you're talking to her and asks what you said. You tell her that you were talking to Susan but your friend says that there's no one else shopping in the store. You turn back to the woman and she's gone but there's no way she could have just vanished like that. What do you do in these instances? When it comes to seeing spirits, you should take a minute to analyze what Susan just said to you and see if there is a deeper meaning to the conversation than you initially thought. You may find that there was, or it may seem random and only be revealed later. Let's take it one step further. Say you buy a blouse and at the checkout your friend teases you about seeing Susan. The lady at the checkout looks surprised and asks for details. You tell her and then she says that her aunt Susan just passed away. While the conversation you had with Susan didn't have a specific meaning for you, it had deep meaning for the employee.

Sometimes you'll pick up information about total strangers when you weren't even trying to read them, and the feeling is so overwhelming that you have to say something. You'll know when you're experiencing that kind of strong impression because it completely fills you with the compulsion to talk. Once I had this kind of impression when standing in line at a checkout. I kept hearing that I should tell the person in front of me that Mary was okay. I didn't know if I should say anything to her or not and I held back until I just couldn't anymore. I told the lady that she'd probably think I was crazy, but I have intuitive abilities and I needed to tell her that Mary was okay. If it meant nothing, I was sorry to have bothered her. To my surprise, she burst out in tears, grabbed me, and hugged me tight. Mary was her daughter and she'd recently died in a car wreck. She'd been asking for a sign that her daughter was okay. The message I'd received was very important to her, the sign she'd asked for. So you'll have to play it by ear when you receive messages like this. Act when you feel compelled to and keep quiet if you feel you should. If you're receiving more information than you can handle, block some of the energy around you with a shield of white light and ask your guides to filter it more.

Intuitive Band

No, I'm not referring to a musical band of intuitively gifted people, even though that would be pretty cool. An intuitive band is a feeling of pressure on the body that occurs when you're developing your abilities. You usually feel this band around the top of your head but it can also occur over your ears, eyes, or chest depending on which ability you're trying to develop. Not everyone who develops their abilities will feel this band but if you do, rest assured that it will go away once you're feeling secure in your ability.

When I first realized that I had abilities, I occasionally felt tightness around the top of my head. I didn't know what it was at the time so I didn't know what to do to make it go away. The result was a lot of headaches. Now that I understand what was happening, I'm going to pass this along so that if you experience the same thing, you'll be able to prevent headaches, or any other pain, while developing your gifts.

The reason that you get an intuitive band is because you are unconsciously holding in and controlling the higher frequencies that you're accessing when working on the ability instead of allowing the energy to move in its natural flow. In my case, I was working on clairvoyance, which is centered in the third-eye area and the top of the head. As I practiced, I was inadvertently holding the energy in one place instead of letting it flow freely. When Universal Energy isn't allowed to move, it builds up and can cause pressure or even pain. I'm frequently asked about this by intuitives who suffer from headaches after doing a reading. I used to be one of them but once I discovered that the energy had to flow continuously, the headaches stopped. Other intuitives often get tired after doing readings. Or if you're working on clairaudience, your hearing may feel muffled afterward. It's the same principle. Your energy feels drained or you feel like you can't hear as well because while you're connecting to Universal Energy, you're not allowing your own energy to flow in harmony with it.

To prevent intuitive bands from happening, make sure that before you start the work, you intend that your energy flows harmoniously with the Universal Energy in an even, smooth manner. Imagine both energies as two rivers running side by side, each maintaining its individuality but occasionally merging to form a creek between them. The impressions that you pick up are the creek. Then when you are finished with your work, imagine the creek dividing and going back to its respective river, thus maintaining the flow of each energy pathway. By doing this creative visualization exercise along with your intuitive development work, you release any pent-up energy and don't hold it inside. If you notice that you're still feeling an intuitive band after you've finished your intuitive work, then take a few moments to connect to the ability you were working on and look for any excessive energy that you unconsciously held on to. Let it go and you'll find the pressure of the band leaves, too.

Hesitation

You may not think of hesitation as an intuitive sign, but oftentimes it's your ability stepping in to keep you from making a mistake or taking inappropriate action. Hesitation centers in your stomach region and the upper body; it makes you stop in your tracks, suspend your words, while giving you a moment to think about the possible outcome of what you're doing or are about to say. It can make you catch your breath, lose your train of thought, or trip over your words. It can cause your stomach to clench and your heart rate to increase. Hesitation is often accompanied by fear. You may be afraid to commit, trust, succeed, participate, do or be involved with something, or even freely state your opinion. Hesitation can occur at any time, so when it does, pay particular attention to what is going on around you, the people you are with, and the root cause of what made you hesitate.

Sometimes hesitation is followed by an intuitive impression and other times it is caused by the impression. Let's say you're speaking with an individual and you're being asked to do some volunteer work that you really don't have time to do, but you want to help out. As you're about to say that you'll do it, hesitation comes over you and you get the impression that if you do this, you'll end up working much longer than you anticipated and it will interrupt an event that you had planned later in the day. So instead of accepting, you offer to volunteer at another time but not on the specific day requested. Is there any way to know for sure that volunteering on that particular day would run into your evening plans? No, you'd only know for sure if you participated and it happened.

If you hesitate but don't know why, scan the area and yourself with your intuitive senses to look for the reason you've been given pause. Is there fear involved? Or is there something else going on? You may pick up an impression that makes perfect sense and then again, you may not get anything at all. And that's okay. If you're hesitating, there's a reason for it, so hold off on making any decisions or commitments until you've had more time to think it through, for the impression to manifest, or for the reason to become apparent.

Gut Instincts/Gut Power

On a soul level, you know everything. On the physical plane, you don't. Your gut instincts are the soul's way of guiding you along your life path, helping you to know right from wrong, good from bad, and which path to choose. There is power in the impressions you receive because they guide you so well. I also refer to this type of ability as gut power. You will always take the right path and make the right decisions if you always listen to your gut power, your instincts, and your intuitive guidance. When your gut power kicks in, so do your intuition and clair abilities, all of which work hand in hand to help you on your soul's journey.

Let's take a look at some examples of gut power at work. It's Friday night and you're meeting up with a bunch of friends at a local restaurant to have dinner before going out to a theatrical performance. The tickets were bought months ago and it's an event that everyone in your close circle of friends has been looking forward to attending. At the restaurant, you order cheese fries, oysters on the half shell, and pork chunks as appetizers. When the food arrives, everyone digs in but you get the impression not to eat the pork, so you don't. Later on, everyone who ate the pork starts to get sick. In this case, because you listened to your gut instincts, you had power over your decision and prevented yourself from becoming ill.

Your gut power can also be expressed through physical manifestations. You may get a tingling sensation all over your body, sweaty palms, sudden sleepiness, and butterflies in your stomach. Your claircognizance may kick in and you just know, without knowing how you know, that you should or shouldn't do or say something. You may get a physical sign in conjunction with your gut instinct. Let's say your favorite bird is a cardinal. You're driving on the interstate and going a bit too fast when you get the impression to slow down immediately, so you do. Then a cardinal flies through your field of vision, and then moments later, another car swerves into your lane just ahead of you. Had you not slowed down, they would have hit you. That's one wreck you avoided by listening to your gut power and intuitive impressions. It is very important that you become aware of these physical signs that the Universe is giving for you to pick up through your intuitive impressions.

Your gut instincts can also help you notice lies, danger, illness, potential problems, those you want to help, favorable outcomes, and areas in which you will excel. They are there to guide you in both good and bad situations.

Sensory Overload

Experiencing frequent sensory overload is one of the ways you can tell that you have intuitive abilities. Because you are intuitive, you tend to feel and sense emotions, loud noises, and other stimuli more than someone who isn't in tune with their abilities. Negativity feels like it's ripping you apart and joy can feel a thousand times multiplied. You feel loud noises in your skin; you're anxious, nervous, and unsettled. This is especially true for those of you who are empathic. Being in a crowd drives you nuts, makes you feel claustrophobic and ill at ease. The chaos of a chain retail store on a Saturday afternoon during a major sale is nearly impossible for you to handle. You feel like you absorb the energy of those around you, letting their emotions affect your mood; you hear information about them as you walk by, see visions about things they've done or will do, or simply know information from an intuitive perspective that you really didn't want to know. You find people are drawn to you and will just walk up and start telling you about all of the things that are bothering them—private, personal information. You tend to make your shopping trips short and during times when other people may not be there or you become a homebody who rarely leaves the house. You avoid watching the news on television or any type of real-life drama because you're affected in the same way.

Living like this can be very upsetting and aggravating if you let it, especially if you don't understand the reason it's happening. That's why it is so important to learn to protect yourself by putting up specific barriers around you. Having intuitive abilities is a wonderful gift, but it's important to learn how to understand them, control them (as much as they can be controlled), and use them while protecting yourself from an onslaught of intuitive information.

I've already explained how to protect yourself with white light, so now I want to share another method that will help you. You could just avoid anything that sends your emotions into overdrive, but then you'd be living a life of isolation and loneliness, which is a waste of the life you've been given. You should live life to its fullest, not hide away from it. Instead of withdrawing from life, in this creative visualization exercise you'll use a switch, a cast-iron suit, invisibility, and fire to keep you balanced in hectic, sensory-overload situations.

There is one thing I want to clarify before I tell you how to do this exercise. Your light will always shine brightly because you are a spiritual being who is able to utilize more than just the five senses. People will be drawn to you simply for that reason. When this happens, while you might not want to hear about someone's surgery or problem with their home, you may receive an impression that will help that person in some small way. So be open to those who approach you and always be nice. Your kindness and words may make a world of difference in their lives.

Try It Now: Intuitively Handle a Crowd

Let's do this creative visualization exercise with the example of going to the store during a big sale. Before you enter the store, you're going to imagine that you're wearing a thin suit of living cast iron that, once you step into it, molds to your body and becomes part of your skin, covering every inch of you. This cast iron is so strong it keeps all negativity from reaching you. It has reflective ability, making sound bounce off of it before you really notice the things said, unless someone speaks directly to you. Program the cast iron with these intentions prior to its first use. Now that you have your armor on, you're going to surround yourself within a ring of fire a specific distance away from you. This ring moves with you, so if you program it for five feet, then it will keep people at least five feet away from you. If you really don't want someone to talk to you, use creative visualization to keep others from noticing you by placing an aura of invisibility around yourself. All of these things are controlled by a master switch and sub-switches. As you near the store, turn the switches on, focus on what you've created, and enter the crazy sale-day world. As you move through the store, you can try turning off specific switches or making your distance ring smaller. You might even try turning everything off except the cast-iron suit, just to see what happens. You'll find that the more you practice, the better this exercise will work and soon it will not be needed at all. It's basically using creative-visualization techniques and tools to help you manage your abilities.

Physical Signs: Headaches, Vibrations in Body

Intuitives are called "sensitives" because they are easily affected by the energy around them, whether it comes from other people in the form of emotions and feelings or from the physical and spiritual worlds. I'm going to go over some of the physical signs that you may experience in association with your intuitive ability, but make sure you always rule out any possible medical problems before assuming that the condition is related to your intuitive ability. I wouldn't want you to really be sick and ignore it.

Now, that said, let's look at some of the symptoms you can experience due to your intuitive ability. For me, the worse symptom was headaches. I had to learn to tell the difference between a tension headache and one brought on by abilities. I went through a period of time when my abilities were developing so fast that I seemed to have a headache all the time, especially those ocular migraines that cause your vision to go out but you never get the actual pain in your head; you just can't see while it's happening. As I learned to fine-tune my abilities, I started doing more work with energy. That's when the headaches started to go away. I still have them every now and then, but the ones I have now are not always caused by my abilities but are more often stress related.

Working with your intuitive abilities, especially when you're trying to develop them, can often cause fatigue, weakness, and an overall feeling of exhaustion. I'm always asked if I get tired from doing readings. I did often get tired when I first started doing readings, but now I'm at a point where readings generally don't faze me. I've learned to separate my physical energy from the energy I use when I'm doing readings so that I'm not exhausted. I'm also at a higher frequency than I was when I first realized I had abilities. The higher your frequency (your personal energy vibration), the less you are impacted physically. If I'm doing online workshops and posting several hundred times during the day, then I'll get tired from the actual typing, but not from doing the readings.

As you work with your intuitive abilities, you may also notice moments of dizziness or lightheadedness prior to a experiencing an increase in your frequency. You may also have vision issues prior to seeing a clairvoyant vision, or you may experience a ringing in your ears before hearing a clairaudient message. When I first started having visions, my physical vision would become blurry; then I'd see what looked like a television screen that had gone off the air, with either snow or squiggly lines, prior to seeing the actual vision. This was how I knew that what I was seeing would indeed happen.

As you become more comfortable in your abilities, you'll find that the physical symptoms lessen because you learn to recognize your abilities without experiencing the physical manifestations.

People Crowding Your Personal Space

One of the situations that goes along with being intuitive is the fact that people are drawn to you. They feel a need to be in close proximity to you. Because of this, you'll notice that your personal space can be invaded quite often.

Your personal space is the amount of area around your body that you feel is yours. This amount of space may be larger with strangers and smaller if you're with your significant other; there are many variations in between. When someone steps into your personal space, you may feel very uncomfortable. It can feel like aggressive or passive behavior, but it's disconcerting either way. Different situations will also affect the amount of personal space you require.

Most people who step inside your personal space are attracted by your positive energy and light. They are comfortable with you and feel at ease when next to you even if they don't know why; they may not even realize that standing so close to you is bothering you. You can step back only to have them return into your space. It can be that your light, your intuitive awareness, is enabling them to feel grounded and centered when they are close to you. This doesn't mean that they're psychic vampires—people wanting to be close to you to draw on your energy to energize themselves—it only means that they like you and feel a connection to you. As an intuitive, you have to learn to tell the difference between those who unconsciously need to be close to you because they're drawn to your light and psychic vampires (see "Psychic Vampires" in chapter nine). The first will do you no harm, the second will. There are also people who purposefully enter your personal space to "help" you by projecting their energy to you. You do not need anyone's energy but your own. If you feel this type of invasion, you should immediately surround yourself with white light and block that person's attempt to change your energy or your aura and politely leave their company.

Because you are intuitive, you feel, see, and know more than someone who isn't in tune with their abilities. When someone invades your personal space, reach out and do a quick analysis to see if they are just insecure and feel drawn to your light. I tend to allow a person to stand close to me, even if I feel uncomfortable with it, if I sense that they are drawn to my light. If I step back and they follow, then there is a reason that it is happening and I won't step away again. It may be that you will act as a catalyst to help that person in some way, whether it's gaining insight into intuitive abilities, spirituality, or just giving them a confidence booster that they need. To be honest, this was a difficult thing for me to learn to do; I like my personal space to be clear of other people unless I want them there. It may be hard for you as well, but if a person's reasons are pure, you may choose to allow their closeness.

Difficult to Surprise

I love being surprised, don't you? Especially when it's a good surprise that takes me completely off guard. The problem is that I'm difficult to surprise because of my intuitive ability. You may be the same way. If you're the kind of person that is hard to surprise because you always know what's happening no matter how sneaky everyone tries to be, then you are intuitive, even if you don't think you are. When you're intuitive, even a small glance between those trying to surprise you will be full of impressions, and you'll know.

For me, parties are the worse. I always know. I sense what's going on long before it happens and I really don't like knowing because I love being surprised. So I try to put up blocks near holidays or birthdays so I don't pick up on what's going on, but it doesn't always work. The very best surprise party that I ever received was when I was pregnant with my youngest child. My husband took us shopping for a new baby bed even though we had a perfectly good one. I started getting tired—I was about to burst with baby at this point in my pregnancy and wanted to go home. But my husband wanted to do this and that (after the fact I knew that he was stalling). We finally got home at 12:30 p.m. We parked the car, got the kids out, and he and the kids walked into the kitchen through the garage door in front of me. When I walked in, all I heard was a loud "SURPRISE!" All of my friends and family were standing in my dining room and sunroom. There was food everywhere and a huge stack of presents for the new baby on a table. But there wasn't a car anywhere to be seen in front of my house. I'm laughing as I write this because they had all parked on another street on the other side of the neighborhood and walked to our house. My mom and husband knew too well how hard it is to surprise me, so they'd been in super-stealth mode for several weeks. I hadn't picked up on a thing. It was the coolest baby shower ever, one that I'll never forget, simply because it was such a fantastic surprise.

If you find yourself in the hard-to-surprise club with me, recognize that your intuitive abilities are the most likely cause. You can put up blocks that keep you from picking up on the surprise. It doesn't always work, especially if your abilities are strong, but when it does, it's absolutely wonderful.

Getting the "Chills"

As an intuitive, you often connect with signs from the Universe that let you know you're on the right path or are fulfilling your life purpose. You may experience déjà vu or you may clairvoyantly see an event unfold that acts as confirmation. If you ask for a specific sign, that sign is often delivered. The most amazing sign that I've ever experienced is what I call the Chills of Universal Truth. These chills are not unique to me; everyone experiences them many times in their life. The key is to know what they are, so that when you do experience them, you can fully understand their meaning.

The Chills of Universal Truth are different than any other chill you will ever experience. You may catch a chill while chilling at your friend's house, watching a movie that gave you the chills, or a documentary that sent chills up your spine. But the Chills of Universal Truth is an all-encompassing feeling that signals you have hit upon a Universal Truth that surpasses this lifetime and penetrates to the depths of your soul. You will probably speak your amazed wonder out loud with a "whoa" or "wow." There isn't any way to avoid recognition and acceptance of what you've experienced because the feeling is too powerful and overwhelming to ignore.

How do you know when you're experiencing this? Let's say you're talking with your friend on the phone and you're discussing intuitive abilities. You doubt your abilities and she's being a sounding board as you let your feelings out. During the course of the conversation, she says to you, "Don't doubt yourself. Remember that the essence of the soul shines through, regardless of whether or not you believe you're doing everything right." Your friend just thinks she's giving helpful advice but as she finishes her sentence, you know, utterly and completely, without a single doubt, that what she just said is a soul truth *for you*. Suddenly you understand that your intuitive abilities don't have to manifest exactly like everyone else's; you just have to do what feels right to you, because this is your life path and your truth. As these thoughts flash through your mind, Chills of Universal Truth start at the center of your being, energizing you, completely filling your mind, body, and spirit. The feeling moves out to your extremities—your arms have goose bumps, but you feel an odd sense of security through every fiber of your being. Sometimes you shudder as the Chills of Universal Truth race through you. Other times, it is followed by peaceful warmth. You feel empowered with the knowledge you've just gained; you have connected with your soul truth and are filled with light awareness.

When you experience a chill of this magnitude (and you're not standing outside in ten-degree weather), think of what was said immediately prior to the chill encompassing you. It will be connected to your soul's truth in some way. Usually the words themselves will seem to stand out so you notice them prior to getting the chill. They may seem louder or grab your attention if you were only half listening to the conversation. These words were meant for you; they are yours, embrace them.

Strong Reaction to a Stranger

When you meet someone for the first time, you decide whether or not you like that person based on your first impression of them. You look at how they present themselves, how they're dressed, their hygiene, and what they say and how they say it. You also base your opinion of the person on how they come across to you. Are they confident or a know-it-all? Do they seem genuine or fake? Sometimes you may make the wrong decision because you really don't know the person well enough yet, and over time, they could prove you wrong. Maybe the person has had a horrific day or they're sick. There could be extenuating circumstances that cause them to make less than a good first impression. Then again, your first impression may be correct.

Whether you realize it or not, you also make your decision based on your intuitive impressions of a person at your first meeting. You may have a strong negative or positive reaction to a person that you don't understand. When your gut reaction is extremely strong, whether it's positive or negative, you're picking up on that person's energy and intent;.it is also possible that you recognize them from a past life.

You should always listen to your first impression, even if you end up being wrong. Keep it in the back of your mind until the person proves to you that what you initially sensed was incorrect. It only takes one time of getting burned by disregarding your first impression to make you wary. In my life, I've had three instances that really stand out and because of them, I always pay attention to my first intuitive impressions when meeting someone. The first time, I met a person who gave off such intense negative vibrations that I ended up quitting my job. Three months later, the company was out of business due to the actions of this person. Another time I met a person and it was like cats circling, ready for a fight. We didn't like each other at all. But, during a visit to a medium, a past life was revealed that explained it all and we went on to be friends until life took us our separate ways. The third time, I got a strong negative reaction and didn't act on it. Months later, there were major problems with this person and it was discovered the person had a drinking problem.

Intuitive impressions that you receive during your first meeting with someone should never be ignored or put up to your imagination. In all three cases I just mentioned, my empathic ability gave me the ability to feel these individuals' negativity. In some of these situations, the negativity can be resolved; in others it can't.

Sudden Urges

One of the ways your psychic abilities can manifest is in sudden urges. Out of nowhere, you might abruptly feel that you have to go somewhere and do something. There are no if, ands, or buts about it. You feel that you absolutely must follow the urge. The feeling is very strong, as if you're being guided to do this thing, and it's usually your spirit guides helping you. If you do what you're being urged to do, you'll often find that you were "in the right place at the right time" and good things resulted from your actions, which makes you happy. When you ignore these sudden urges, you'll probably discover something later that lets you know why you felt the way you did.

Sudden urges often happen when you're driving. Here's an example of a time when I received a sudden urge and ignored it. I needed to go to the feed store, which is about twenty minutes driving time from our barn. Five minutes of that drive is on a major interstate. As I was driving toward the interstate, I got the sudden urge to take Central Boulevard instead of going on the interstate. It would take an extra ten minutes of driving time. I decided just to take the interstate—boy, did I regret not listening to that sudden urge. I had just exited the ramp and driven about a minute when traffic came to a complete standstill. I sat in traffic for nearly a half hour, creeping toward my exit. Had I taken Central, I would have saved myself a lot of time. That just goes to show you that intuitive impressions in the form of sudden urges will help if you'll listen to them. It might not make a lot of sense at the time, but will most often be clear later.

Let's look at another example of how this can work. What if you got the sudden urge for ice cream? How could that have anything to do with intuition? Isn't it just a craving? Let's say you act on the urge to go get ice cream. You're sitting in the ice cream parlor munching away on a yummy banana split when in walks a friend you haven't seen in months. You invite her to sit with you, and find out she also had a sudden urge for ice cream. During the conversation, you find out about a job opening at the company where she works. Because you've just been laid off, she offers to put in a good word for you. The next week you're back to work and spending more time with your friend. So that sudden urge to get ice cream was in fact guidance for the two of you to reconnect and for you to find a new job. Now aren't you glad you went to get ice cream?

Hunches

A hunch is an intuitive feeling that you get about a situation. It's different than a sudden urge where you feel compelled to take immediate action. A hunch can pull at you, nag at you until you either take action or disregard it. You may find out after the fact that your hunch was correct and you might regret not acting upon your feeling, or it may have been wrong and you're relieved. Either way, following your intuitive hunches is a good way to strengthen your intuitive ability. The more often your hunches turn out to be right, whether or not you have chosen to act on them, the more you will trust in your intuition.

Following a hunch is not out of the ordinary. Business people follow their hunches all the time and usually don't attribute them to any type of intuitive ability. However, it is their intuition at work. Making decisions and taking risks based on hunches often turn out to be correct.

Another aspect to consider is how often you have hunches. Do you get them on a daily basis or only once in a blue moon? The more attuned you are to your hunches, the more you're accessing intuitive ability. You may find that other people consider your hunches to be fascinating and will wonder how you know these things. Other people might say that you're lucky or that you are so logically inclined that you can figure things out before they happen. Only you know if you're being overly logical or tapping into your intuition. You might even be doing a little of both.

Let's look at a fictional example. You're in a meeting at work and you notice one of your coworkers is often glancing at his secretary. She glances at him quite often too, and then you catch the two of them sharing a secretive smile. Logically you think that these two must be having an affair. The woman sitting next to you leans over and whispers, "I have a hunch that we're all in for a big surprise." You think to yourself that their spouses will have an even bigger surprise when the truth comes out. The meeting continues for over an hour and you've forgotten about your assumption. Then, as your boss is finishing up, he says he has a big announcement to make. The door opens and in walks a huge celebrity. Everyone is shocked to learn that your company has just signed a multimillion dollar deal and hired the celebrity as the new company spokesperson. The boss goes on to thank the two coworkers who were smiling so secretively for closing the deal and signing the celebrity. You were wrong and the woman with the hunch was right.

Hunches don't always pan out this way. Sometimes they are wrong. As you develop your intuition, you'll start to feel the difference in the energy of a hunch that will prove to be correct and one that may not turn out as you perceive it.

Déjà vu

Déjà vu is a French term that means "already seen." When you experience déjà vu, you feel as if you have already experienced what you're doing at that exact moment. It can be so overwhelming and strong that you know exactly what will happen next. Sometimes it does happen and sometimes it doesn't; the unique aspect of déjà vu is that you shouldn't be familiar with the situation you are experiencing, yet you are. You're happily going through your daily life when suddenly a few moments in time feel as if you've already lived them. It stops you in your tracks, and you feel very strange. Almost everyone who has this experience will voice the experience at the moment it happens by saying "déjà vu." It's such a common saying that almost anyone who hears it will know what is happening to you.

There are many different hypotheses as to why déjà vu occurs, from medical issues to dreams you've had in the past that you don't remember. It's often thought to have nothing to do with intuitive abilities or spirituality. I'm not a medical doctor so I can't voice an opinion regarding medical causes for this phenomenon, but I can give you my opinion from a spiritual point of view and as a clairvoyant. I believe in reincarnation and that we each map out a plan for our lives prior to birth in order to have specific experiences on the earthly plane and to learn lessons from those experiences. Therefore, I believe that déjà vu is a sign that we have also planned on the spiritual plane to let us know that we're on the right path here on earth. It's a memory from when we were on the Other Side and planning our life paths and lessons. We may have planned to experience this memory during difficult times or at random points in our lives as an indication that we're following our life path and are on the right track. It's reassurance that we should keep moving forward, no matter how difficult the circumstances that we're experiencing in our lives. Think about the times when you've experienced déjà vu. Were you going through major life changes? Were you under stress? Worried? Did you experience more instances of déjà vu during these times than you normally do? I've found that this does happen and that déjà vu will often come in spurts. There may be long periods of times between each experience, but during other periods it will happen quite frequently. The closer you are to your chosen path, the more you will have déjà vu, just as you will have it more often during times when you question the reason for your existence and when you need reassurance that you're doing what you're supposed to be doing in your life.

You may disagree with my take on this, and that's fine. That's your path. But the next time you experience déjà vu, consider how it is connected to your life and your intuitive abilities. You may be surprised at what you discover.

Coincidences

Coincidence is defined as "a striking occurrence of two or more events at one time apparently by mere chance." Do you believe in coincidence or that things happen for a reason? Believers in coincidence may still be finding their way on their spiritual pathway, or have yet to see the Universal picture of what is happening in their lives. As they become more spirituality enlightened, they usually see the bigger picture and blame events on coincidence less and less, while looking for the spiritual purpose behind the event. When it comes to coincidence, you may not see the reason behind what happened immediately, but you do look for the reason because you see it as something that you planned to learn or as a catalyst for an event which gives you the opportunity to learn or help someone else learn.

Sometimes the reason for the coincidental thing that happened is immediately apparent and at other times you never learn the exact reason. Have faith in the knowledge that you are moving along your path and the event is part of what you have set out to learn in this lifetime. There is always a spiritual purpose behind what happens to you in life. Try to look for deeper meanings behind coincidental events and your motivation in situations. Find your purpose in the moments as you live them; seek the inspiration of the lessons you are to learn and move forth on your chosen path.

Synchronicity

Synchronicity is when several unrelated events lead up to a specific outcome that has meaning to you. Coincidence, if you believe in it, is when something happens simply by chance and without any purpose. Synchronicities are often messages in disguise. They are experiences created by your higher self or your guides that will bring you greater awareness. Synchronicity is when unrelated events happen at the same time and these events speak to you on a soul level or reveal something that has profound meaning to you. They often feel like they are divinely guided in order to bring you to a place of awareness and understanding that you may not have achieved, had the sequence of events not happened in the way they did.

Synchronicities let us know that we are on the right path by allowing us to learn something that will advance our spiritual growth. There isn't any way to explain why the events happened the way they occurred. Synchronicities have a positive effect in your life, because they influence and expand your thinking. They can bring about what you need—people whom you should be in contact with or awareness that wasn't within you before the event.

Cloud Messages

A *cloud message* is exactly what it seems; when you look up at the sky and see a cloud in the image of something that has meaning to you, it is confirmation of a question you've been pondering or is enlightening in some other way. A cloud may be in the shape of a personal symbol, an angel, or even appear as spelled-out words. Cloud messages are often a sign that a spirit is near and communicating with you.

Receiving a cloud message is different than just trying to find fun shapes or pictures in the clouds with your kids or a friend. They are more dramatic, they make you think on a spiritual level, and you feel or sense a message associated with them.

If you're faced with a problem or need confirmation of any kind, ask for a cloud message. Then take your camera so that you can record what you see. Find a place where you can sit quietly and look at the sky, watching the clouds. When you see one that feels like it's drawing your gaze to it, take pictures. Cloud messages don't usually last very long due to the atmospheric winds, so pay close attention.

Try It Now:
Find a Message in the Clouds

For this exercise, head outside to a park bench or somewhere you can sit quietly. Take your camera and a notepad so you can take pictures of the cloud messages or draw them if you don't get pictures in time. As you sit in your chosen spot, think of a question or situation you want answered. Now watch the clouds to see what forms. Write down or photograph the results, making sure to write down how you feel about the message. You will hopefully find this information very valuable when you go back and read it later.

....

Were you able to recognize some of these subtle ways that your abilities present themselves? You may have more of your own experiences that you can add to this list, things that happen to you that may not have been addressed here. If you haven't started writing down how your abilities appear and how they work for you, now is a good time to start. By keeping a written record instead of just relying on your memory, you'll be able to look back and see your progress.

Five

Using Your Abilities in Everyday Life

Most of you will probably decide not to work as a professional intuitive and give readings for others. Instead, you may be an "everyday intuitive" and use your abilities daily—to gain insights into situations where you need assistance, to offer support to others, or to generally guide you as the unique individual that you are. In understanding how your abilities work by engaging them on a daily basis, you will spread your light among those you meet and interact with daily. By connecting with your own abilities, you may inadvertently help someone else connect with their unique abilities. Embrace the intuitive part of yourself as you live life. Your abilities are a gift to guide you on your spiritual path.

When you're in tune with your intuitive abilities, they can be very helpful in your daily life. You can learn to fine-tune them so that they can be used at a moment's notice without requiring you to sit in a special place using specific tools. Take time to practice working with your abilities without a routine, using them randomly throughout the day. Becoming comfortable using your abilities may take a little time, but through focus and practice it will become second nature to you. The following are examples of ways you can begin to actively incorporate or recognize your intuitive abilities in your everyday life.

Parking Spaces, Clearing Phone Lines

Sometimes life can be frustrating. Having intuitive abilities can also be frustrating because you don't always want to know the things you know, and when you do want to know something, it might be totally evasive. But there are times when having psychic abilities is hugely beneficial. You can see right through someone who isn't telling the truth, you know what is going on when people are whispering and keeping secrets around you without having to be told, and you can open up parking spaces during the rush of the holiday season (or at any time that a parking lot is full and you need a space). Don't believe me? Well, here's how you do it.

If you know ahead of time that the parking lot will be packed (for instance, if you're going to the mall on Black Friday), then use creative visualization and imagine yourself driving to the mall and finding an empty space on the first row you drive down. You can also ask your guides for help, especially if you arrive to find that there aren't any empty spaces. Just ask them to clear a space for you and lead you to the open spot. You'll often find that one opens up right away. Remember to always thank your guides when this happens.

The next time you make a phone call and get a busy signal repeatedly, use your intuitive abilities and the power of manifestation to imagine a clear line so the call will go through. Using your third eye, which is located in the center of your forehead between your hairline and the bridge of your nose, you'll clairvoyantly look at the connection between your phone and the place you are calling. If you're using a cell phone, visualize the signal traveling through air; if you're using a land line, envision a big black cable filled with other multicolored smaller cables. As you focus on this connection, send strong positive energy through the line to clear it. Imagine that all of the stagnant energy that is clogging the path moves out of the way, allowing your energy to quickly clear a passageway for your call to connect. This is not kicking someone else off the line so your call can get through. It is visualizing that the line *has cleared* so your call can connect. Now, dial the number again. If you don't get through, do the exercise again and make sure you're using clear focus and very positive energy. I use this exercise all the time and find it works.

You can also use the same method for clearing a phone line to intentionally move something. I'm not talking about telekinesis, although this could be a mild form of that ability. When you move something with intention, you're sending a thought to a person or thing to do something differently than what is currently being done. For example, let's say you're driving on the freeway and you're blocked in with cars on all sides, and they could move into a different lane but aren't doing so. If you really want to get out of this box, send the drivers of the other cars the thought to move into a different lane so you can move over as well, then say thank you when they do. You can use this same technique in other little ways throughout your day.

Receiving Intuitive Impressions for Yourself

I'm often asked if I get impressions for myself. Sometimes I do and sometimes I don't. When you are intuitive, there will be times and certain situations where you don't get impressions for yourself or for those you are extremely close to. If a traumatic experience happens and you didn't see it beforehand, you may blame yourself. I want to address this because I feel that there are people who become fearful of using their abilities because they were wrong in the past or because they didn't see something they felt they should have seen or known.

The thing with intuitive abilities is that you can't always predict what will happen in your own life because it's a conflict of interest. We are here to learn life lessons and to grow spiritually in order to progress on our life path, so how can we learn anything if we're always seeing everything that is going to happen to us? Sometimes you have to live the experience to learn from it. You're also so emotionally involved with what is going on in your own life that you sometimes can't see the situation clearly. After all, you're only human and this is part of the human experience.

That being said, there are plenty of times when I have seen things for myself or my loved ones. When I worked outside of my home, I'd look in the newspaper for work whenever I was looking for a job. I always knew which jobs I'd get because it looked as if the words would rise up from the page like a little three-dimensional picture. I'd apply and get the job. I do readings for myself all the time, I talk to my guides, and I follow my impressions. It's normally the big things that I don't see for myself—the things that really put a strain on life like accidents, sudden illnesses, or financial crises. If I'm not seeing a situation clearly, I'll ask a trusted psychic friend for their impressions to see if I'm totally off base or if what they see fits with what I sense.

No psychic is ever 100 percent correct. If someone tells you they are, don't get a reading with them. Don't expect that you will see everything that will happen to you and those you love. That's an unreasonable expectation. You can be intuitive, help others with your abilities with love and understanding, and still learn the lessons you need to learn for your own growth. Don't beat yourself up about what you didn't see; instead, learn whatever lesson the event held for you. Don't throw your abilities away but rely on them and know that you will be shown what you're supposed to know. Ask for guidance from the spiritual realm and then listen to the advice you receive.

Finding and Eliminating Fears with Intuition

Fear is the one emotion that will continually hold you back in all areas of your life. But it doesn't have to be this way. You've probably heard the saying that you should "face your fears," but how do you do that if you're afraid? It's not easy, but if you use your intuitive ability to search out the source of those fears, then they're easier to face and eliminate.

Growing up, I always had an abnormal fear of ants and false teeth. Go ahead, laugh. These were really irrational fears but to me, they were very real. All I had to do was see a set of false teeth on television and I'd burst into a fit of uncontrollable crying. Let an ant get on me and the same thing would happen. Everyone laughed at me, said I was being silly, and they were right, but I didn't know how to stop the reaction. I thought the reason I was afraid of ants was because, as a baby, I'd been sitting beside a tree and ants got all over me. I didn't even remember it, but I'd been told about it growing up. I was afraid of false teeth because someone in my childhood told me they were going to give me a present so I should close my eyes and hold out my hands. I did, and when I opened my eyes, there were false teeth sitting there. I screamed, dropped them, and hid under the porch. It was very traumatizing for me.

I decided to use my intuitive abilities to try to get to the bottom of these fears. I asked my guides to help me and to show me the source of the fear so that I could eliminate it. I used my clairvoyance during meditation to sense the instigating event for these fears. Boy, was I surprised to learn that the fear of ants had nothing to do with ants getting on me as a baby, but it stemmed from a past life. Once I saw this past life and understood my role in it, I was able to release my fear of ants. I still don't like those little creatures but I'm no longer terrified of them.

The false-teeth fear did stem from the event that happened in this lifetime, but I realized that it wasn't because of the false teeth, although it was shockingly traumatic to see them in my hands. It was the fear of trusting someone and having that trust crushed by an adult who thought it was a funny practical joke on a ten-year-old child. There wasn't anything funny about it to me. By looking back at the event as a stranger looking in and using clairvoyance to help me see it clearly, I was able to understand and let it go. I still don't like false teeth but I can look at them now without emotion.

You can face your fears in the same way by searching for their root cause with whatever intuitive abilities you possess. Ask your guides for their help. Once you find the cause, you can take back the power it's holding over you and let your fear go.

Intuitive Triggers

An intuitive trigger is the ability to set physical signs as reminders for something you need to do, or to set exact symbols for spirit contact, upcoming changes, and growth of intuitive abilities. You may have used your ability to set intuitive triggers for yourself without even realizing that you did it. This works on the spiritual level just as tying a string around your finger to remember something works on the physical level.

The first type of intuitive trigger is one you use to remind yourself of something you have to do. For instance, you have a doctor's appointment at 4:00 p.m. on Tuesday. You might intuitively set a trigger that you'll see an orange frog three hours before the appointment to remind you of it. Then, when you see that orange frog on the television, you remember your appointment. This works because you're using your ability to set and program a specific reaction to the energy of a specific catalyst. The catalyst can be anything you like: a gallon of milk, an animal, the ringing of a bell, or even a stapler. It doesn't matter what the item is, it's your choice, and the energy connection to the catalyst is what activates the memory of what you need to do. Granted, with the technological advances in cell phones, you may not need an intuitive trigger to remind you because you could just set an appointment alarm to ring, but if you're working on advancing your intuitive potential and strengthening your abilities, then try using this type of trigger for a while instead of your cell phone. Make the trigger something out of the ordinary that you wouldn't expect to see. If it's a common occurrence, then it may not work as well.

The other type of intuitive trigger is one that, when you see it, you know it is a sign that a very specific type of intuitive experience is about to happen. You can set different triggers for different types of phenomena. You may have a sign that your spirit guides show you every time they are going to communicate with you or to let you know they are nearby. It may be a butterfly, a dove, or a specific number. Or you may experience a whirring sound in your ears to let you know you're about to astral travel, you might see an angel formed in the clouds for angel contact, and you may encounter a different sign that lets you know you're going to have an experience that will lead to the development of a new intuitive ability.

Regardless of the types of intuitive triggers you set for yourself, using them will allow you to remember, become more aware, and feel a greater connection to your own abilities, guides, and spirituality.

Try It Now: Set an Intuitive Trigger

For this exercise, I want you to choose an event that is coming up this month. Once you have the event in mind, sit quietly and choose an intuitive trigger for it. For this exercise, choose a butterfly to be the trigger. Once your trigger is set by following the instructions above, wait until the event happens; once it has happened, write down the details of the event and how the trigger worked for you.

Validation Signs/Confirmation Signs

While intuitive triggers always happen before the event, confirmation signs happen after the event to let you know that what you experienced was indeed intuitive or spiritual in nature. I see dragonflies all the time regarding intuitive experiences. Or, if I'm talking to someone, I may see confirmation signs for them. Something that will confirm to them that what we were discussing is part of their truth.

Whether you're just beginning to learn about your intuitive abilities or are a longtime practitioner, there will be times when you will receive validation signs in regard to your intuitive gifts. These are second signs that act as confirmation of a previous sign or impression that lets you know the information you received was correct.

When spirits are around, they will often give you signs of their presence. Your spirit guides, angels, or loved ones who have passed often use signs to let you know that they are with you. Loved ones may send a particular scent, song, or specific words that were important to them in life or that meant something to the two of you. Angels often have unique scents or will leave feathers to let you know they are near. Specific objects such as coins are also used. Sometimes you may not understand that what you're experiencing is a sign. You may notice the sign and think of your guide or loved one, but not realize that the sign is from them, so they will send you another one until you connect the dots.

It's easy to question your intuitive talents and doubt that you're correct in what you're experiencing. Your doubt will lead to a second sign from the spiritual plane that lets you know you're right. Let's look at a couple of examples. Let's say you're cooking dinner and you've got the television on in the adjacent room. All of a sudden someone on the television says the words "knee high to a grasshopper." Those words seem to jump out at you and remind you of something that your grandfather used to say when he was alive, so you go into the other room to see what the show is about. It's a news anchor reporting on a story. As you look at the television, the reporter's name pops up in a little box near the bottom of the screen. The reporter has the same first name as your grandfather. This is a validation sign that your grandfather is close by. So you go back to the kitchen to finish dinner and realize that you're cooking pork chops, your grandfather's favorite meal.

When it comes to intuitive impressions, they can happen in a similar manner. Let's say you suddenly sense that you need to go to the store for milk immediately, even though you still have half a gallon in the fridge. So, following your impression, you jump in the car and go. On the way there, you notice a sign that has the words "wait until tomorrow" on it. In the store, a lady you don't know starts to talk to you. She's telling you, a complete stranger, about a problem that is worrying her. You think of the half-full milk carton and the words that you noticed and you tell her, "Sometimes you have to look at the glass as half full, and sometimes, you just have to wait until tomorrow for the situation to become clear." The woman suddenly smiles at you and says, "You're right. That's exactly what I'll do. I'm sure this will work out just fine." Because you acted on your initial impression to go to the store, and paid attention to the signs that you received along the way, you were able to help someone who was upset to see a situation more clearly. Pay attention to the signs you are given because they have the ability not only to help you, but others as well.

Knowing What Someone Is Going to Say Before They Say It

If you've known what someone was going to say right before they said it, or maybe you said the exact same thing as someone else at the exact same time, that's intuition. Let's look at a couple of explanations as to how this can happen.

Sometimes we know one another so well that we're able to finish sentences or even communicate with just a look. But isn't this also intuitive in nature? I believe it is. We might be so in tune with the other person that we just know what they will say next. People that are this close often finish one another's sentences.

Sometimes, we do not know the person at all. When you're able to finish the sentence of a person whom you do not know, this is an example of your intuitive abilities at work. You clairvoyantly pick up on what they are about to say seconds before they speak the words. You're briefly connecting with their energy and with them on a soul level.

If you had a nickel for every time you knew what someone was going to say before they said it, or for every time you said something at the same time as someone else, I bet you'd be rich, wouldn't you? Finishing sentences for someone else or knowing what someone is going to say before they say it are signs of your telepathic ability shining through.

This doesn't apply to talking over someone, which is finishing what you think they're going to say just because you're too impatient to give the person time to talk. When you do that, it has nothing to do with psychic abilities. You're just interrupting them. Talking over someone is telling them indirectly that you think they're inarticulate and you don't have the time, interest, or inclination to listen to what they have to say. If someone is struggling for a word and asks, "What's that word? It's on the tip of my tongue," that's a request for assistance and if you answer then, you're helping them out.

Your telepathic ability comes into play when you either think the exact same words at the exact same time as they are said by someone else, or you verbalize those words and both of you say the same thing. Then one of you says, "Jinx! You owe me a soda," and have a good laugh. This normally happens more with people whom you're close to than strangers because you're more in tune with their energy and have a connection to them. Best friends or twins sometimes only talk in half sentences because they already know the rest. A conversation between telepathic people who are this close can be difficult to follow. Sometimes, they can just look at each other and know what the other one is thinking. That is a true telepathic connection.

Mind-Over-Body

Sometimes called "mind-with-body," this is when you are able to control your body's sensing abilities and physical reactions by focusing intuitively on the energy surrounding you and using visualization to positively affect it. This is not a predictive type of ability where you're receiving impressions. Instead, you're using intuition to connect to your energy. I've been fascinated with this concept since I was a teenager and saw a documentary about a man who could consciously slow down his breathing and heart rate so much that people thought he had died. Of course, after the show was over, I had to try it. In order to control your body in this manner you really have to intuitively tune in to every fiber of your being. You must be at one with your breath, heart, and blood flow. You must feel a connection to your intuitive and spiritual self and you must maintain a firm control over the way your body reacts to your intuitive suggestions. It's always good to have someone with you when you try an exercise like this. Then they can monitor your success rate. If you are breathing at twenty breaths per minute and you're able to slow it down to eight, or you're able to reduce your pulse from ninety to seventy, then your abilities are working to control your body as you're instructing them.

People also use intuitive mind-over-body techniques to control pain or heal wounds. When women are in labor and the medical staff says to find a spot on the wall, focus on it, and breathe, you're essentially calling on your intuitive self to control the pain by focusing elsewhere. You can also focus directly on pain to bring about faster healing. The next time you have a small cut, intuitively send healing energy to the pain of the cut, giving it the intention that the cut will not hurt anymore and will heal in half the time it would normally take. Write down your results.

People who find themselves in exceptional life-or-death circumstances will fall back into their primitive intuitive nature to push back the need for sleep, food, and even water by connecting to their soul essence in order to survive. I've seen numerous television shows where people have talked about imagining their body being warm from the inside out when caught in extremely cold weather. This is using intuitive focus to keep your body going, without feeling pain or cold during the experience. Some will say that this isn't an intuitive ability because the people who can do this don't label themselves as intuitive. Many in the medical field will say that this cannot happen because the body heals itself without any influence from the mind. That's absolutely true, but I also believe that giving intention and focus through the use of our intuitive healing abilities can bring about positive results in the form of faster healing. Other people, while under a doctor's care, have obtained miraculous results through the power of prayer and by using their intuitive nature to heal from within. Sometimes you just have to have faith and believe. In doing so, you open your soul essence to ignite your own healing abilities.

Unblocking Intuitive Energy

We all have had days, or periods of time in our life, when everything that could go wrong did go wrong. Do you feel like you're unlucky, as though fate has it out for you and it's just your destiny to experience negativity? If you're experiencing these types of situations, it is likely that your intuitive energy is blocked. You're no longer in sync with your abilities; when you're intuitively out of tune, you feel stuck until you can find your way back to center. This is sometimes easier said than done. You may not notice any self-sabotaging things that you're doing to clog and backup your intuitive channels. You may subconsciously feel you deserve what you're getting, that you're not seeing the forest through the trees, and you may feel as if nothing will ever change in your life. Is there a life lesson that you're supposed to learn but you're just not getting? If your intuitive energy is blocked, this could very well be the case, especially if you feel that you've unblocked yourself but are still experiencing the negative situation. When you're not in tune with your intuitive self, it's easier to miss the lesson behind the situations befalling you.

So how do you unblock your intuitive abilities so you can become more grounded and in tune with this part of your essence? You let go. Release all the negativity in your life. Make changes, let go of what no longer serves you, and find your way back onto your life path instead of drifting around in the woods and fighting the undergrowth at every turn, making little progress with these obstacles.

You are in control of your destiny; your destiny does not control you. You're only unlucky if you think you're unlucky. Remember, like attracts like; if you're always thinking you're unlucky, then you'll continue to be so. Fate means that something was predestined to happen in a specific way. You are the creator of your life path; you put these situations in your way to learn something from them. Clear your mind, focus your emotions, and take time to examine what the lesson is.

To unblock your intuitive energy, the first thing you have to do is realize that it is blocked. If you avoid or ignore it, then you'll be stuck in this pattern. Next, you have to release any negative energy that has accumulated within your person or environment so you can move forward again. Start by using white light to cleanse yourself from the core outward. Then acknowledge it by saying out loud, "I am in control of my destiny." See your intuitive abilities as separate pieces of yourself and cleanse them. Once you've done this, you'll find that your flow is clear and strong and you are able to reconnect to your soul essence of being. Imagine yourself grounded to the earth, centered and focused. Now that you've unblocked your abilities, connect to their positive energy each time you use them.

Your Abilities and Water

Sometimes you can receive intuitive impressions or moments of great spiritual insight about your abilities when you're taking a shower, soaking in a bath, or relaxing in the pool. Some intuitives even do readings with water and get impressions from the way it swirls in a cup or the way droplets form on a glass; they may dip their fingers in the water and then let it drip from their fingers onto a flat surface and do the reading based on how the droplets are arranged. Water is a great conductor of impressions for many reasons. Before we were born we lived in water; when we are connected to it now, we relax and feel comfortable, making it easier to receive impressions or messages.

Sometimes when you're blocked intuitively, water can unblock you. I'd like to share an exercise that I often tell people to do that will help them connect with their intuitive abilities, relieve stress and anxiety, and allow them to release any negative energy surrounding them. It is a simple exercise but its benefits can be substantial.

Try It Now:
Unlock Your Intuitive Abilities with Water

The first thing you'll do is run a deep, hot bath, not a lukewarm or cool bath. Get the water as hot as you can stand it without burning yourself. If you want to put fragrance into the water, that's perfectly okay because it will help you tune in even more. Stand in the tub. Now (because the water is hot and your skin is sensitive) *slowly* lower yourself into the tub. As the water flows over your skin, imagine its energy flowing into the muscles of your legs and all the way through your body as you sink deeper into the water until you're submerged up to your chin. Visualize the water's energy flowing through you, seeking out any negativity and soaking it up like a sponge. Ask your guides for any messages that they want to relay to you; think about new ideas you would like to create or solutions to problems you need to resolve and then let these thoughts go. Clear your mind, feel centered within yourself, and connect to your own intuitive energy. Now, and this is the most important part, *relax*. Soon you will begin to receive solutions, new ideas, and insightful messages. When you are finished soaking, imagine the energy of the water that you drew inside of you now moving out of you, taking any negativity with it. Stand up in the tub at this point and pull the drain so that the negativity doesn't reattach to you. Shake any water off of your feet as you get out of the tub and dry off. Then write down any messages that you received while soaking. When you're stuck, this exercise can give you a new perspective on things. You'll feel recharged, invigorated, and more in tune with your intuitive nature.

Sensing Trespassers

If you've entered a space that no one but you is supposed to have access to, such as your home, workspace, car, or any other part of your property, and are overcome with the sensation that someone else has been there even though nothing is out of place, then that is your intuition warning you. When you psychically connect to this sensation, you know right away that it was a living person that invaded your space. To me, this feels like a heavy, prickly sensation of the energy of the intruder. Sometimes you can determine exactly who it was and other times you can't. This sensation is one that feels persistent and gives you a sense of uncertainty.

When your intuitive abilities are on high alert in these types of situations, you should always pay attention. More often than not, the person is someone you know, a coworker or a family member. When you start asking around, you will discover the cause of your sense of unease. Other times, it may be someone you don't know and who isn't supposed to be there. Recently I've had this sensation at our barn. Something just seemed off, as if there was an energy that didn't belong. Over the course of several months, it started as small things. Feed bins and stall doors were unlocked when I knew for a fact that I'd shut and latched them the night before, items were in the wrong places, and then it escalated: the tail of one of our horses was cut and there were injuries that just didn't make sense. Because of the impressions that I'd received, I became more alert and aware of how the barn looked at night and anything that was wrong in the morning. We started calling the police and filing reports. I notified everyone in the community, put signs on the property, and lit the barn up with floodlights so that anyone who came into the barn would be seen. I double-checked everything twice at the end of the day. Soon the feeling went away and we no longer had any problems. Had I not been in tune with the energy of the barn as well as my intuitive connection to my animals and their behavior, this intrusion may have continued. So make sure that when you have these types of feelings, you tune in intuitively, focus, and become more aware. It may not be anything serious, but then again, it could be warnings that will help you head off future problems.

Other times, you may sense that a person is in your space when you're expecting them to show up. You look, but they haven't arrived. In this case, they are projecting their energy to their destination before they actually get there, and because you're waiting for them, you pick up on this energy. When this happens, you'll find yourself constantly looking out of the window to see if they've arrived because you're picking up their projected energy.

Finding Lost Items

If you're particularly good at finding things you've lost or that someone else has lost, then you're probably using your intuitive ability to find the missing object. This is a very helpful way to use your abilities, especially if you're running late and have misplaced your car keys. Let's look at some ways to use your specific abilities in order to find missing items. If one method feels blocked to you and isn't working, try using a different ability to locate the object.

When an item is missing, it's easy to get frustrated and anxious as you attempt to find it. Instead of letting your emotions get the best of you, stop. Stand still for a moment and focus your attention on the object. Use your clairvoyance to seek out the energy of the lost item and then see yourself finding it a few minutes into the future. Now go to where you saw yourself finding what you've misplaced. More often than not, it will be where you saw yourself finding it. If you're empathic, you'll do the same thing. Stop, focus on the object, and feel its location. Walk around the general area until you feel drawn to a specific spot that just feels right. If you are clairaudient, ask your guides to tell you the item's location. Listen carefully and then go look in the place that you hear.

You can also use remote viewing to find lost objects. First, think of the object that has gone astray, and then follow the energy path of the object to its current location. Similarly, creative visualization can be used to find lost objects. Imagine that you're intuitively connected to the item by a cord of energy. Now gather the cord in your hands, gathering it up as you walk closer to the object. When you're out of cord, you'll find the item.

One thing to remember is that sometimes you're not supposed to find the lost item, but instead you're supposed to learn a lesson from losing it. There are times when the thing that you've lost has served its purpose for you and has been found by someone else in order to fulfill a purpose in their lives. Let's say you have a favorite worry stone, one of those little polished stones that you keep in your pocket and rub when you're worried, and then out of the blue, the stone is missing. The lesson in losing it could simply be that you've grown past having to rub a stone to eliminate worry. You no longer need this device so your worry stone has been lost, only to be found by someone who needs a worry stone. If the item is supposed to remain in your life (like your car keys), then you will find it easily by using your intuitive abilities.

....

So how did you do? Were you able to incorporate the use of your abilities in your everyday routine? If some of the methods I discussed seemed difficult, give them a fair chance to work and take what feels right to you in these practices; if something does not feel right, you may not be ready for it at this time in this life. For those practices you are meant to have in this life, you'll soon connect with the ability and be able to use it whenever you need it. Don't give up. Your abilities are a core part of yourself. They are intertwined with your soul, a clear knowledge and a gift to be treasured. Embrace them.

Six

Types of Abilities and Psychic Experiences

Everyone is born with intuitive abilities and we use them daily, even if we do not identify them as intuitive. We are all individuals who charted our lessons and level of growth prior to this lifetime for specific reasons. Each one of us moves along our spiritual path at the rate that is right for us. Once you become comfortable with your abilities, new ones will continue to emerge when you are ready. Think of it this way: you couldn't learn everything presented to you from kindergarten to twelfth grade overnight, and neither can you master your abilities overnight. Intuitive abilities are part of your spiritual growth. Therefore, you will progress when the time is right for you.

Some of you may know for sure exactly what your abilities are, while others may wonder whether your experiences are just products of a vivid imagination or something more. So how do you tell if you have abilities or not? Maybe you've had an inkling for a while now. You know things before they happen without having any reason to know them. This is clairvoyance. Sometimes when you walk into a room, you feel like you're being watched from the upper corners—greet those spirits in the corners as you pass by. Maybe you even see shadow people walk by who aren't there when you look again. Do you realize that you just saw a spirit? You hear your name called when alone (your guides do this a lot), you smell odors and aromas that have no physical source (from a recently departed loved one), and the light bulbs in your house are constantly blowing out (spirits trying to get your attention).

All of the things I've mentioned above are just some of the ways you can tell that your intuitive abilities are at work. You will be experiencing these things with one of the clair abilities or through your mind's eye. While physical manifestations do occur, they are rare compared to the daily manifestations you will experience through the third eye.

As you learn about what you can do, you must also learn to trust yourself. My biggest problem is always self-doubt. When I do a reading, I always wonder if it was accurate. I pass the information along as I receive it and hope that it is relevant to the person's life and situation. I never know if it is or isn't unless they write me back and tell me. But it is this self-doubt and worry about my accuracy level that keeps me from getting an inflated ego.

How do you know when you're having a metaphysical experience? In this chapter, you'll discover a variety of methods and presentations that will let you know whether what you are experiencing is intuitive, spiritual, or paranormal. Consider each of them, note if you've already had a similar experience, and keep in mind those experiences you haven't yet had so that you will recognize them when they appear in your life.

Intuition

Instincts are part of our human existence. Intuition is the psychic part of our instinctive nature. It is the ability to obtain knowledge or have a belief without being able to justify it. It comes from a place deep within you and there isn't a way to logically prove what your intuition tells you. A well-known example is "a mother's intuition." Think back to your own childhood. How many times did your mother know you were doing something that you weren't supposed to be doing? Or if you hurt yourself and she came running out of the house to check on you at just that moment? As a young adult, your mother may have called you out of the blue when you were feeling lonely, upset, or were trying to make a difficult decision. I jokingly tell my kids that "moms know everything" and while they're quick to point out that I don't know everything, they can't argue with my mother's intuition. We all have this kind of intuition, whether or not we have children. It applies to friends, family, acquaintances, and situations.

The more you acknowledge your intuition at work, the more it will grow. By paying attention to the times you listen to your intuition, and you witness the results that follow, you will grow more confident. Your intuitive nature isn't based in fear, so you should analyze how your intuitions feel so that you know the difference between feelings of fear and intuitive impressions. Feeling fear unrelated to intuition is different from your intuition warning you and then feeling fear after the intuitive impression.

What does intuition feel like? It is a deep resonating sense that feels like it comes from the depths of your soul. It may lead you to check on a loved one just to make sure they're okay or to make decisions that just "feel right," even though someone else may question or disagree with your choice. If your intuition is warning you away from a situation or person, it may feel like a barrier rising between you. If it is guiding you toward something that will help you, it may feel like a positive energy guiding you, even if you don't understand why.

The most important thing in understanding and developing your intuition is recognition. When your intuition feels true to you, when you feel certain that you're on the right path (even if that path is a warning) and you accept it as such, you're embracing your intuition. Sometimes your intuition will conflict with your feelings. If it does, then your intuition is probably the path to follow. If you're considering relocating to a new town but your intuition is telling you to stay put, then don't move. Wait. Maybe the time isn't right. The reason that you shouldn't move will probably become apparent if you just give yourself a little time before acting on your feelings.

Intuition leads you in the right direction. It gives you a clear understanding of what form your abilities might present themselves. When reading through the following types of abilities, pay attention to what you most relate to and what might be manifesting in your life. Again, as you progress in time, new abilities may pop up. It is good to learn about each so you can recognize them when they appear.

Extra Sensory Perception (ESP)

Extrasensory Perception (ESP) is when you are able to obtain information without using any of your five senses of sight, hearing, taste, touch, or smell. ESP is using your "sixth sense," including any and all of your intuitive abilities, to obtain information that you should not know. ESP is first and foremost a way of communication using the sixth sense and focuses mainly on clairvoyance, telepathy, precognition, retrocognition, and psychometry, but it's not limited to these five abilities. ESP is a broad term that covers all aspects of intuitive abilities from remote viewing to clairvoyance to astral travel. I'm including the term ESP in this book because not only is experiencing any type of ESP a sign of your abilities, but this term is also how many people describe the sixth sense.

When one thinks of ESP, what often comes to mind are lab tests where an intuitive predicts the shape printed on a card (these are called Zener cards) or other testing methods. This study of ESP is called parapsychology. In the field of parapsychology, scientists try to prove the existence of intuitive abilities through scientific methods. While the research has made great strides, there has yet to be concrete proof that abilities exist.

Once you realize that you have some form of ESP, the way you can increase the abilities is to practice regularly. Extrasensory perception has been with you since birth and will be with you until the day you die. Everyone has it and you can increase the strength of your abilities through practice. Becoming more accurate in your ability is similar to an athlete practicing for an athletic event. The more athletes run, the faster they become because they have conditioned their body to surpass itself during every workout. The more they use their muscles, the stronger they become over time. It's the same way with your intuitive abilities. The more you practice and acknowledge your abilities, the stronger they will become and the more accurate you'll be in your knowledge and in any predictions you may make.

Prophetic Dreaming

There are many different types of dreams. Some dreams are just your subconscious working through things that happened during your day. Nightmares or very busy dreams that have weird and strange things happening at a quick pace can be the result of eating spicy food prior to going to bed. However, some dreams have greater meaning, and their purpose is to reveal something new to you. You can learn a lot about your dreams through dream interpretation. There are many books on the market that will tell you what each aspect of your dream means. When you combine all of the symbols and meanings together, you can interpret what the dream is trying to tell you. Then there are prophetic dreams, which are completely different.

In a prophetic dream, you will normally see a future event. These dreams usually have specific qualities about them that, over time, will help you separate them as unique and prophetic. If you always dream in black and white, and then you dream in color, this could be an indication that this dream is prophetic. I always know when my dreams are prophetic because they feel completely different from other dreams that I have. I always dream in color, but in a prophetic dream, the colors are so vibrant they almost seem alive. I am always an observer in the dream, usually watching it from above or from the sidelines as the scenes play out. I always feel like the dream is real; I hear people speaking and I feel the elements.

When you have a prophetic dream, it can be a warning of an upcoming event that you can take action to change when you realize that the dream is happening in your life. Other times, there's absolutely nothing you can do about it. Sometimes these dreams show you joyous occasions and at other times, the events aren't happy. Let's look at a couple of examples. The night before the Oklahoma City bombing, I had a prophetic dream where I saw massive rubble and huge chunks of concrete lying everywhere, and I heard children crying and people screaming. The dream didn't last very long, and those elements were all that I remembered, but it was so traumatic and real that I woke up crying. In this case, there wasn't anything I could do. In another prophetic dream, I saw myself driving a red car and going around a curve. I noticed a particular tree, out in the middle of a field. There was a motorcycle with two people on my side of the road coming right at me and we crashed head-on. Then a couple of days later, I was coming home from work in our red car, noticed the tree in the field, remembered the dream and instantly braked my car, slowing down to about twenty miles per hour and moving toward the middle of the road. Sure enough, a motorcycle came flying around the curve, went past me on my right instead of the left and out into the field. I pulled off the road and ran to check on the driver and passenger, who had both been thrown from the motorcycle. Luckily, everyone was all right. In this case, because I acted on what I saw in my prophetic dream, a car wreck was avoided and no lives were lost. Had I not slowed down and moved over, I have no doubt that the prophetic dream would have happened exactly as I saw it.

Lucid Dreaming

Lucid dreaming is when you consciously realize that you're dreaming during the dream. You can become lucid at any point during a dream. It often happens when you notice something outside of the realm of the physical earthly plane that seems impossible (for instance, if you suddenly grow ten times larger than your normal size), while at other times, lucidity is just a sudden realization that you're in a dream. It is a skill that you can develop. One way is to give yourself a symbol like a mirror, a horse, your hands, or a cell phone. Look at that symbol (or a picture of it) before you go to sleep and tell yourself that when you see that symbol in your dream, you'll realize that you're dreaming.

In a normal dream, you will just accept whatever happens in the dream. If you're lucid dreaming, you can make deliberate choices and actions. In the lower levels of lucid dreaming, you are aware that you're dreaming and can alter what happens in your dream. If you're in the middle of a nightmare and a monster is about to eat you, then you will feel real fear; if you're lucid and know you're dreaming, you can choose to fly away out of its clutches. At the lower levels, you may not realize that everything you're dreaming is happening in your mind or that you're asleep in your bed. In the higher levels of lucid dreaming, you are aware that everything you're seeing, feeling, and participating in is created in your mind; you know that you're safe, and sleeping peacefully in your bed, and will awaken at some point. By knowing what lucid dreaming is, and how to influence your dreams, you can effectively put an end to nightmares if you become lucid during them.

Once you're aware that you are lucid in a dream, you can intend to do specific things such as flying, going on adventures that you create, or coming up with innovative ideas and concepts. You can also ask your spirit guides to come to you and have a discussion with them. This is where your intuitive abilities come into play. It is commonly thought that seeing a deceased person can be the catalyst that lets you know you're lucid, because you know the person isn't living on the earthly plane. While this is true, I believe that, once lucid, you can have discussions with the people you love that are now on the Other Side. You can also obtain precognitive answers to questions or access the Akashic Records (see "Akashic Records" in chapter seven), all during your dream. It's easier for spirits to contact us in the dream state because we put up barriers when we're awake that block them. If you're lucid, you'll be able to obtain more information from spiritual sources and those on the Other Side. The possibilities are endless.

Astral Projection/Astral Travel

In order to astral travel, you must be intuitively in tune with the etheric world and the planes of existence around you. The astral plane is similar to the earthly plane because it contains everything you find on earth: people, buildings, roads, etc. However, you don't experience the basic physical needs of eating, sleeping, or going to the bathroom. Each of us has an astral body that we can use to travel within the astral plane. During travel, we remain connected to our physical body by a silver cord of energy. When astral traveling, you can move at the speed of sound or take a casual walk. You can astral travel for specific reasons, and if you choose to visit the upper levels of the astral plane, you can gain a greater understanding of your own spirituality, intuitive abilities, lessons for this lifetime, and divine soul purpose. Astral projection, also known as astral travel, is when you intuitively will your soul to leave the physical body and go into the astral plane. While in this dimension, you may visit other places or people in the physical realm.

Try It Now: Astral Travel

Let's go over the basics of how to astral travel. Try not to make this more difficult than it is. Sometimes, simpler is better when it comes to techniques. Choose a time when you will not be interrupted to lie down somewhere comfortable and clear your mind. In order to project your astral body into the astral plane, you have to have a great deal of focused concentration and be in a light trance. Your body should feel heavy and paralyzed, unable to move, while your mind is wide awake and ready to travel. The quickest way I've found to get to this state is to imagine every muscle in your body relaxing. As it does, imagine that you're sinking into the object you're lying upon. Feel it wrap around you, keeping you safe. Now, raise your frequency from within by focusing and drawing upon Universal Energy. Feel it enter through your crown chakra (located at the top of your head), energizing you from your core outward. When you feel ready, imagine that you're stepping outside of your physical body and into the astral plane. See the silver cord that attaches you to your physical body. You may hear a buzzing or whooshing sound as you do this. Explore the astral plane at length; when you're ready to return to your body, imagine the silver cord retracting, drawing you back to your physical body. Once you're out of the trance, make a point to stand up and ground any excess energy by sending it from your body through the bottom of your feet, through any flooring underneath you until it goes into the earth.

Remote Viewing

Remote viewing is the ability to access information from a remote geographical location—allowing you to see people and events that are going on in the present but are outside of your physical range of vision—using something other than the known five senses. If you have this ability, you may be able to describe faraway places that you've never visited or people whom you've never met or seen before simply by using remote viewing. The remote viewer can be in North Carolina and see an event happening in Japan at the very moment they are looking with their intuitive ability. Some people think remote viewing can be taught and you don't need any kind of intuitive ability to do it. However, I believe that in order to view that which is outside of your range of physical sight, you have to use the clair abilities on some level.

Typically, remote viewing isn't used during readings or to tell the future. It is structured, scientifically based, and usually done in a controlled environment. This was especially true when the United States government got involved in training remote viewers in the early 1970s. It takes time and a lot of practice to become a highly skilled remote viewer. When you're conducting a remote-viewing session, you must put away all preconceived notions of what you think will happen and instead, without any kind of bias or wandering thoughts, put yourself in the moment and focus on the "target," even when you don't know what the target is.

Can you be a remote viewer? Sure you can. There are exercises you can do now to test your skills and decide if remote viewing is something that you'd like to pursue with your abilities. If you look online, you'll find a lot of different remote-viewing tests where you will focus on a target and then a picture of the target will come up on the next screen. A far better way is to have one of your friends or family members cut out some pictures and put them in security-lined envelopes so you can't see the picture. If you've selected ten photos, your assistant should number them from one to ten. Next make a list on a piece of paper. Taking your time, focus on the picture inside envelope number one. It you pick up a word, write it down; if you see a scene, draw it. Even if you only see lines, draw them. Do a remote-viewing session on each envelope. Then, when you're finished, take the pictures out one by one, comparing them to what you wrote or drew. Were you close? You may have gotten the general lines of the picture or you might have drawn it perfectly. For example, if the picture was of a lake with mountains in the background and you drew several inverted *v*'s with a circle below them, then your session was successful. You detected the primary lines within the photo. With practice, you will find that you will be able to correctly draw or describe more details of the photo through remote viewing.

Visions

A vision can take you by surprise; on the other hand, if you're doing a reading, you may expect to see them. They can be brief, fleeting glances of something that is going to happen, an event that has already happened in the past, or they can go on and on like a movie and you see specific details. They can occur when you have your eyes opened or closed and they appear to be projected in front of you like a movie on a screen. Some visions will move from the right to left, or the left to right, or appear directly in front of you. Visions always give you needed information about someone or something; the information can be for you or someone else. Often it's up to you, using your intuitive ability, to decide what the vision means and whether or not you should act on it. It's not always easy to experience visions. Some can be graphic, or they can be things you really don't want to know. There's always a reason that you're seeing them, but some of them can leave you with uncomfortable feelings and nag at you after the fact.

When you experience a vision, you may not be sure of it at first. You may second-guess yourself, doubting that what you've seen will happen or that it is true. But then, in time, you might discover that what you saw was exactly right, that an event happened just as you saw it happen in your vision. When this pattern repeats over and over again, you as an intuitive will start to know that what you're seeing is true and real.

Visions are useful tools that every intuitive uses. As an intuitive, you can practice having visions. This will help to further develop the ability so that when you receive a spontaneous vision, you will recognize the truth in it and know how you should react. Many people will choose to try to have a vision during meditation. You can also take a simpler approach by just asking your guides to "show" you something very specific, a past life for example. Then pay particular attention to the vision as it plays out. If it's a past life, then see if there are facts from your vision that you can check out to confirm that what you saw is correct. You can also test your ability to see future events in a vision by asking a specific question. You might ask if it will be sunny or rainy tomorrow, or you could ask if you'll have unexpected visitors over the weekend. Write down what you saw in the vision. Then, when the time has passed, compare what you saw in the vision to what really happened.

Psychography/Automatic Writing

Using your mediumistic abilities, you can choose to participate in automatic writing to receive messages from entities and spirits. The information received can be meant for you, someone you're reading for, or the world in general.

There are two methods in automatic writing. The first type is when a spirit is inside your body; the second type is when a spirit is outside your body and communicating telepathically. In both methods, you should protect yourself with white light prior to beginning the session. This will prevent negative energy from attaching to you.

In the first method, you will go into a trance and the spirit or entity enters your body or part of your body (your arm and hand) to write the message. You are unaware of what was written until after the fact. Some mediums choose to use the second method, where the spirit doesn't enter their body or use their arm, but instead gives guided messages telepathically that the medium writes down or types. It's like dictation. The spirit talks and the medium writes or types. As the medium, you can choose to go into a light or deep trance or to be a conscious channel while the message is written. I am a conscious-channel medium, which means I'm fully conscious and aware during the reading, and use all of my intuitive senses to receive the information from the spirit; however,

I will sometimes go into a light trace if I'm having a difficult time hearing the spirit (the light trance makes it easier to hear soft speakers). I type as I'm receiving the message.

The text created through automatic writing on paper seems to have one unique factor: the pen is never lifted from the page and there is a line connecting one word to the next. This is important to know so that you can tell the difference between automatic writing conducted by a spirit and regular human writing. Sometimes there may be perfect punctuation and other times the words are misspelled. The writing may be in your handwriting or one that you don't recognize.

What are the benefits of automatic writing? If you are a grounded, well-practiced medium who understands how this tool works for contacting spirits, then it can be used to contact your spirit guides or higher-level spirits. However, there are causes for warnings against using this method. I cannot stress enough that if you do not know what you're doing when it comes to psychic and paranormal experiences, then you should seek the advice of someone who does have the knowledge and experience and who can make contact for you instead of trying to do it on your own. They will take protective measures and they can teach you how to do things correctly. It is dangerous to delve into the spirit realms when you don't know what you're doing, and it could result in lower-level negative spirit attachment. In helping others along their path, I have experienced these kinds of situations firsthand many times.

It is important that you don't become addicted to conversing with negative spirits through automatic writing sessions. This can cause you to create a bond with them, which allows them to attach to your energy. For this reason, it is important to protect yourself with white light before the session. It is also not advisable to believe everything you read from your automatic writing. You may be in contact with a lower-level negative entity who is pretending to be your guide. Using your intuitive ability of clairvoyance to search out the truth is an imperative step that must be taken if you want to pursue automatic writing. The people I know who did automatic writing without knowing what they were really doing had problems for many years, and may still be having problems today.

Automatic writing is one way of using your psychic abilities that I would avoid unless you know what you're doing and it's a natural progression in the development of your abilities. Some guides or departed loved ones will communicate in this manner, but it happens only when the intuitive is at a point in their development where automatic writing is the next logical stage. An intuitive should not just decide one day to let any spirit hop into their arm at random. A choice like that can lead to problems.

Spontaneous Drawing

I can't draw well, but I like to doodle. When I'm talking on the phone, or especially when I'm on hold waiting for the person to come back on the line, I find that I'm drawing all kinds of shapes on some piece of paper that's nearby. I'm not consciously thinking about what I'm drawing, I'm just doing it. At some point in my doodling, I realize what I'm doing and look at the mess I've made all over the paper. At times, these doodles may create a picture that holds an impression for me or the person I'm talking to on the phone. Other times, they're just doodles that hold no meaning whatsoever.

Your connection to your clairvoyant abilities can still come out on paper while you're gabbing away on the phone. When this ability occurs, you're usually not consciously thinking about any specific problem, but a solution may show up in the drawing because you're clairvoyantly connecting to Universal Energy and the solution. Artists who paint may experience this same type of event in their paintings.

You can do spontaneous drawing with purpose by focusing on a specific area of concern or interest and then letting your mind relax, connecting with your abilities and core energy, and drawing. It takes a little of the spontaneity out of the exercise, but you can still obtain results. When you do attempt this with purpose, you have to make sure you're not allowing the thinking part of your mind to interfere and you're relying on your clairvoyant nature. It's easy to get distracted and lose the connection if you suddenly notice the lines in the picture and think that it is starting to look like something specific. If this happens, you'll have to start over because the image you create will not truly be clairvoyant but will be a product of your creativity.

Another way that spontaneous drawing can be beneficial is that it hones your abilities, strengthening and manifesting them in a physical way on paper or canvas. You can also do spontaneous drawing with the purpose of doing a soul portrait. This is best done with colored pencils or paint because your soul/chakra colors will become apparent. If there are areas of concern, you can work on them. Before you begin, connect with your higher self and your guides. Tell them what you're attempting and ask them to help you portray your soul in the most accurate way. Then follow your feelings and don't try to interpret what you're drawing. Just draw. Change colors when you feel the need to do so. You might draw yourself, or an image that is a plethora of color and light. When you are finished, look at the drawing to determine if it portrays the deepest feelings within your soul.

Psychokinesis/Telekinesis

Psychokinesis, also known as telekinesis, is a rare ability. It is being able to move, manipulate the properties of, or change the appearance of tangible objects by using only your intuitive abilities and your mind. You do not physically touch or use any kind of force upon the object in any way other than the power of your mind and the strength of your ability. There is no sleight of hand involved—otherwise it is a magician's trick and not true psychokinesis. There aren't many people who can demonstrate true psychokinesis, although everyone has psychokinetic potential. You'll never know if you're one of those rare psychic talents until you try to move or bend something purely by using your mind.

How do you go about it? Because psychokinesis is thought to happen at higher levels of consciousness, you have to connect to that part of yourself by using your abilities prior to beginning. There are plenty of online games that test your psychokinetic ability but I feel it's better to try this using a physical object placed in front of you. First choose the item that you are going to try to move. It could be something small like a playing card, a CD, matches, or anything that is small and lightweight. If you experience success, you can move on to heavier items and bending silverware later. Take a moment to clear your thoughts and really focus on connecting with your higher consciousness and the intuitive part of yourself. Now move this focus from inside yourself to the object you want to move and then ask it to move. Demanding that it moves or wishing it would move isn't the way to go about this. You're creating a deliberate flow of energy between you and the object on a subconscious intuitive level. You're giving this flow of energy a specific intention to move the object. So focus and ask the object to move. Try practicing every day for a while to see if you have success. Try not to block yourself by thinking that you'll fail. If you think that, then it's not going to work. You create what you think, so believe in yourself. You just might be surprised at the results.

Dowsing

Dowsing is the ability of an intuitive to connect to the energy frequencies within the earth through the higher self by using a divining rod to locate water, minerals, gemstones, and other buried objects. It is also known as rhabdomancy, radiesthesia, water witching, witching, doodlebugging, or divining. In order to practice dowsing, you use a dowsing rod, which is often a *y*-shaped branch from a tree. Some dowsers prefer one type of tree over others, willow often being a favorite. I was taught to use a willow branch as a child. Other dowsers use *l*- or *y*-shaped rods made of metal, or a pendulum. The dowser knows when they've hit upon an object under the ground because the point of the *y*-shaped diving rod will turn downward toward the earth. The *l*-shaped rods will cross over themselves using an *X* to mark the spot. A pendulum will move in the preprogrammed direction for "yes." Dowsing can be used to locate lines of positive energy within the earth as well as negative energy lines. If you locate negative energy lines, you can effectively move them using dowsing rods.

In order to dowse, you have to intuitively connect to your higher self and to the energy of the divining rod, giving it a telepathic intention to find the object you're seeking. You can do this by feeling your intention going into the rod, by clairvoyantly seeing it happen, or by visualizing your intention being fulfilled. It is my opinion that if the dowser isn't able to connect with the energy of their higher self and the divining tool, then it will be difficult to locate the objects they are looking for or to obtain answers to their question. I remember my grandmother telling me that I had to *feel* the water in order to find it.

When using a pendulum, hold the end of the chain or string with your thumb, index, and middle fingers. First program the pendulum to move in specific directions for "yes" and "no." Once the directions are clear, you're now ready to ask questions and receive answers. You can use pendulum dowsing to locate lost items. If you're using a hollow pendulum to search for something like water, gold, or gemstones, you can fill it with bits of the item prior to beginning your search. Pendulums can also be used over maps to dowse the location of what you're seeking. The type of pendulum you choose is completely up to you. Quartz-crystal pendulums work very well, but you can use other kinds as well. You may have one you prefer to use when looking for items and another one when asking personal questions. Many people make their own pendulums or use a needle or ring on a piece of string. (See "Pendulum" in chapter two.)

Portrait Clairvoyance

There are two different ways to use your intuitive abilities when it comes to photographs, digital pictures, and portraits. While this is typically called portrait clairvoyance, the way the picture is created isn't important. It could be taken with a camera, painted, or drawn. You may use only one of your abilities or a combination of several, in addition to your clairvoyance, as you receive impressions from the picture. Either way can be effective if it's the way you receive impressions. You should use as many of your abilities as you need to receive the information.

The first method is when you receive impressions by looking at a photo. An acquaintance hands you a picture and says, "That's my wife." You take it, look at the woman portrayed there, and immediately see vivid details about her that have nothing to do with what your acquaintance is saying or the way she is portrayed in the photo. You may feel her happiness and see an image in your mind of her holding a little girl, so you ask how many kids they have. He replies that they don't have any yet, indicating your vision is reflecting a future event.

The second method is when you use your abilities to connect with the entities that help you, your guides, departed loved ones, and anyone else from the spiritual realm that is with you. With this method, you're not going to look at a portrait; you're going to draw one. This is not the same as automatic writing or spontaneous drawing, because you're doing this with intention in order to see and draw those around you. You don't have to be an expert artist to do this, nor do you have to go into any type of trance (although you might choose to). Sit quietly and draw a picture of yourself. As you're drawing, focus your attention on your aura and then expand your intuitive vision and feelings to the area around you. Sense who is nearby and then, using the impressions that you're receiving, draw those around you. If you receive their name, jot it down by their picture so that you don't forget it. Once you've finished your drawing, look at it in detail to see if you recognize anyone from your current lifetime who may have already passed. Do you recognize your spirit guide? If you received names, are any of them ones that you know? New names should be investigated using your intuitive ability. This may be your first introduction to a new guide.

Psychic Photography

Psychic photography is the ability of a psychic medium to capture images of deceased relatives, spirits, and other anomalies on film. During the years that I've worked as a spiritual intuitive, people often ask me to look at pictures that they've taken and give them any impressions I receive about an anomaly that has shown up in the photo—things that weren't visible to the participants or photographer at the time the picture was taken. I've run across a handful of people whose ability to capture spirits on film really amazed me. Their photographs contained much more than the random dust-spot orb (see "Orbs" on the next page). These are the psychic photographers of the world. Once they have a camera in their hands, these intuitives are able to capture astonishing images that even surprise them. If you've ever taken a picture and discovered a strange anomaly, then you, too, are a psychic photographer.

How is it that some people are able to take pictures that contain clear images of deceased loved ones, angels, nature spirits, ectoplasm, full-body apparitions, and other things that can't be explained, some that you don't even know how to categorize? I think that the reason is twofold. First, those who are on the Other Side or who live in different dimensions or planes of existence want us to know that there is life after death, so they show us every chance they get. Secondly, the photographer intuitively connects to the spirit world, which in turn impresses its images within the photos.

Some psychic photographers aren't aware of any changes in the atmosphere around them when they're taking pictures. They just snap away at random during family events or whenever they see something they like and want to remember. It's only when the pictures are developed, viewed on the digital camera's LED screen, or downloaded to a computer that they notice the anomaly. If this happens to you, make sure you write down notes about the event, the names of the people in attendance, and what the conversation was about when the photo was taken so you don't forget later. Other psychic photographers specifically visit places where they think they may be able to pick up spirits on film. If they notice cold spots or a mist while taking photos, they take pictures in those areas and oftentimes something will show up in the image.

If you've ever wondered about this ability, then whip out your own camera, take some random pictures and pictures in areas that are thought to be haunted, and see what happens.

Orbs

Intuitive ability and the paranormal often go hand in hand. When you're intuitive, you have the ability to see, hear, and sense more than what is normal for the physical plane of existence, and this includes the paranormal. Orbs belong to the paranormal realm and most people believe they are the physical manifestation of ghosts, the spirits of the dead. Depending on the type of orb, they could also be nature spirits or as some believe, a completely different life form. You can see them manifest as quick-moving balls of light on this plane of existence and you'll intuitively sense what they are when you see them. Orbs are seen with your physical eyes, not with the third eye. While I have seen orbs manifest in the physical, I tend not to attribute every orb that shows up in photographs to the paranormal.

Orbs often show up in photographs as a white spherical shape. Sometimes they look like they have a darker round circle in the center or slightly off center. The problem with many orbs in a photograph is that most of the time they are not a ghost manifestation on film but are actually some kind of airborne particle that is in front of the camera when the flash goes off, or a dirty lens. Usually this is dust but it can also be pollen, moisture in the air, or even tiny gnats.

How can you tell the difference between dust orbs and real orbs? First, make sure your camera is 35mm if you're going orb hunting. If you're using another type of digital camera, you're going to get a lot of orbs showing up because the dust is being digitized. This doesn't occur as much with a 35mm digital camera, so there's a better chance of capturing real orbs. Real orbs will have a couple of features that dust orbs don't have. They will be brighter—a more solid, white color instead of the thin, faded appearance of the dust orb. They may have a trail of light behind the actual orb, have multiple edges as if they're moving, and you might even see a face inside the orb. Don't confuse this face with the digitized shape in the center of a dust orb. When you see a face in one, you'll also psychically sense that this orb is unique and real.

Seeing orbs physically manifest is different. They may appear as slow-moving orbs; as quick-moving, zigzagging lights; or as unmoving, glowing orbs. When you see this phenomenon, you should immediately scan the lights with whatever intuitive ability you possess and then go with your first impression as to what it is. The lights may feel like they have ghost, fairy, or angel energy. You may also sense that it's your guide trying to get your attention. If you sense something immediately and it's strong, then don't second-guess it.

Try It Now: Pictures of Spirits

Get out your camera and visit a place that is thought to be haunted. Don't worry; you don't have to go in the middle of the night unless you just want to. Visiting the area during the daytime is perfectly fine. If you're uneasy visiting a haunted place, then take a walk anywhere and start snapping pictures of things that you feel drawn to. If you have a digital 35mm camera, you can take hundreds of pictures and then delete them if nothing shows up. Make sure you look at them in a large size on your computer first, just in case you miss something on the small screen of your camera. If you don't own a camera, you can pick up a cheap disposable one at a local store. Sometimes you may catch a white streak or other anomaly that indicates spirit activity. Save those pictures.

Precognition

Let's clear up the confusion between precognition and a premonition before we delve deeper into each one. *Precognition* is a sudden, intense knowing that something is going to happen. In precognition, you often see everything that happens, down to the smallest detail, or you may see enough main parts of the event that, when it happens, there is no doubt that your impression was that specific event. Since no one intuitive can ever know every detail about the future, this ability refers to knowing general outcomes of specific courses of action with occasional flashes of detailed insight. A *premonition* is a feeling that something might happen without being able to determine the details of the event. We will discuss premonitions in detail in the next entry.

Both precognition and premonition have been acknowledged for a very long time. The Greeks used to consult oracles in order to learn about future events. Prophets were also important in ancient times, due to their clairvoyant and precognitive ability to see into the future. Almost everyone has experienced precognition at some point in their lives. Think back to a time when you sensed something that was going to happen in the future and were right about that impression.

As an intuitive, you will gain more confidence in your precognitive impressions by tracking what you saw and the actual results. You can start a log or journal that lists and gives details of each event you saw and the date you received the impression. Then, when the event actually comes to pass, write down the date that it happened. This is important because the event can happen a few minutes after you receive the impression or it may be years later. By tracking the dates of your impressions and the actual occurrences, you can start to see patterns in your impressions. If you notice there are always three days between your impression and the actual event, and it happens that way 99 percent of the time, then you know to expect the event three days after you see it. If the time frames do not have any type of pattern, you'll just have to keep your eyes and ears open to find out when the event happens.

Precognitive impressions can come to you when you're fully conscious or when you're dreaming. They can appear in vivid detail, as a generalized description, or in symbolic form. You may tend to notice that your precognitive abilities happen when you're resting or doing mundane tasks that give the mind time to relax. Precognition is not an ability that you can control. In other words, you can't practice precognition like you can practice clairvoyance. The impressions will come to you when you're supposed to get them and are quite often negative and traumatic events. That doesn't mean precognition doesn't work with positive events. It does. You may see a friend who has had difficulties getting pregnant cradling an infant in her arms and you know it is her child, which is positive. You can also use the information you receive during a precognitive impression to prevent negative things from happening to you. You can, through your free will, change your plans or take a different route to work. At other times, especially when it's a large world event, there's unfortunately nothing you can do to change what you saw.

Premonition

A *premonition* is an unexplainable feeling that something is going to happen when you have absolutely no reason to believe that it will. It isn't as detailed as a precognitive impression and is more empathic in nature. Instead of seeing the actual event happen in detail, as you would in a precognitive impression, you will just know in your gut, on an emotional level, that something is going to happen. You can't explain it, you just feel it. Premonitions are often associated with negative events involving loved ones, such as accidents, financial problems, or relationship problems. You may also receive premonitions about natural disasters, public figures, or major events that the world is watching.

When you intuitively receive a premonition, it is usually accompanied by physical sensations such as an overall sense of uneasiness, depression, unexplained worry, or increased anxiety, which can manifest into actual physical distress the closer you get to the event actually happening. These feelings can sometimes increase in strength until you feel physically sick when you're not ill. A premonition causes you to experience a feeling of constant waiting for the bad thing to happen. When it does, you'll feel a connection to that event and the physical distress associated with the premonition will go away.

Why do premonitions happen? I believe that you are given these feelings so that you can look for potential situations before they happen. Premonitions often warn of danger that can be avoided if you take proper action. They can also prepare you emotionally so an event is less of a shock to your system; we're more emotionally and mentally prepared to handle the situation and offer our support when we've been prepared with a premonition.

You may have premonitions on a regular basis, even if you don't recognize the premonition when you have it. Think of it as subconscious self-sabotage. Let's say you're getting ready for work. You feel a premonition surrounding work but don't realize that you just had a premonition. Suddenly you're not comfortable in your clothes so you change several times before heading out the door. Now you're late. When you get to work, you find the building is shut down due to hazardous fumes being circulated by the air conditioning. Several of your coworkers are headed to the hospital. Had you been on time for work, you may have been headed to the hospital, too. You subconsciously heeded your premonition by making yourself late. At other times, you can consciously use your premonition to avoid a situation. If you sense that you are going to have an argument with a friend, then just avoid seeing that friend until the feeling has passed. Or if you are driving and suddenly get an anxious feeling about the road you're traveling, then exit and go a different way. You may avoid being in a car accident.

Premonitions can also change into precognitive impressions. It may start as a feeling of unease and hours later you're having a full-blown vision of a disastrous event taking place. In these times, keep your cool and let the vision play out, then determine if there is anything you can do to stop what you saw from happening. Sometimes you can help the situation, while other times you unfortunately can't.

Retrocognition

Retrocognition is when you receive impressions, about past events that occurred in this life or in past lifetimes by using your intuitive abilities rather than any physical senses. Also known as "postcognition," it is similar to precognition and premonitions in that it can manifest as a mild feeling or a vivid vision. If you have this ability, you can see, feel, and sense things about a person that they have already experienced. This includes seeing and feeling things that happened in past lives. I've found that when I do readings I will also use retrocognition, and those impressions help to validate the impressions that I am given that have yet to happen. You may see the information playing as if it's a movie, you may see it as though you're viewing through the eyes of a participant, or you may see it as an outsider observing what's happening. You may receive the impressions through vision, touch, hearing, or simply knowing. Any of the clair abilities can send you into retrocognition impressions. Because retrocognition involves events that have already happened, you can check the accuracy of the impressions that you received through research. Granted, not everything you pick up will be documented, especially daily-life types of things, but if you get impressions about events that were well known and documented, then you may discover that your impressions were right. I always think it's a good idea to check out your impressions when you can, because it helps you keep track of your accuracy levels.

I often use retrocognition when I'm doing past life readings. I access the person's energy and then look back into past lives to obtain specific information that happened long ago that can be helpful in their current lifetime. Using retrocognition, I can normally see very vivid details about the people in the scene, surroundings, time, and place and often I even hear conversations. If you were to experience past life recall, that too is retrocognition. You're remembering a past life that you lived and information from that memory will often help you in some manner today. I believe that you're not going to receive information unless there is a reason for it; so always look for that reason, especially when the information comes from the past. Often, retrocognition allows you to find the source of fears so that you can eliminate them.

Retrocognition doesn't always go back to ancient history or times long ago. You can pick up information about something that happened last week, last month, or last year. There are many uses for retrocognition, especially when you use the ability with purpose. You can look for specific information about your current life. For example, if you're terrified of ladders and don't know why, then by using retrocognition you can go back to the point when you first felt that fear. Maybe you were only two years old and a ladder slipped and fell on you. By knowing the root cause of your feelings, you can let them go.

I've heard it said that if you have the intuitive ability of precognition then you can't have the ability of retrocognition. I know for a fact that this isn't true. I have them both and personally know many other intuitives who also do. If you're told that you can't be retrocognitive and precognitive at the same time, disregard that comment; many intuitives can do both, and your abilities are unique to you.

Try It Now:
Use Retrocognition to Remember a Past Life

For this exercise, I want you to stretch out on your bed and get comfortable. Concentrate on using retrocognition to remember a past life that you want to know about at this point in time. Ask your guides to show you this current lifetime as you look for it. Now, with your eyes closed, allow your mind to move back in time to the past lifetime you're supposed to see. Make note of anything that will indicate the time period or the location and pay special attention to the details of the vision. Ask your guides what your lesson was in this past lifetime and how it is related to your current lifetime. Once the vision is over, stretch as you remember the details; then get up and write it all down or type it up so that you don't forget any of the details.

Mental Telepathy

Mental telepathy is when you're able to hear the thoughts of people around you using your sixth sense. It is the ability to communicate mind-to-mind with another person. Physical examples of this happening are when you finish someone's sentence or say the same thing at the same time. Or, perhaps you're out with a friend and find yourself in a situation where you want to leave, and you look at your friend and suddenly *know* to head to the back door instead of the front. When you meet up with your friend a few minutes later outside the back door, you laugh that it's a good thing you're such close friends that you know one another's thoughts.

When people hear the words "mental telepathy," they often think that someone can read their minds instantly, so the first words out of their mouths are "so what am I thinking?" While an intuitive might be able to tell them accurately what they're thinking, I've found that quite often the person who asks that question is just testing you. Mental telepathy is much more natural than the forced "tell me what I'm thinking right now and do it quick" testing approach. By definition, it means that you're using thought transference to communicate with another person without using any of your physical senses. Mental telepathy is associated with intuition and being able to communicate with people who can't speak due to physical reasons. It is also works for communication with your pets and at other levels.

Think of good friends who are able to finish each other's sentences or who don't even need to say a word to know what the other is thinking—one person simply sends a thought to another person and that person responds in kind. Let me give you an example. You've planned to meet your best friend for lunch but on the way there you get caught up in traffic. So you send your friend a telepathic message that you're running late and will be there in fifteen minutes. When you get to the restaurant, you and your friend pull in at the same time. When it's discussed, your friend tells you that she felt that you were running fifteen minutes late so she just arrived when you'd be there. This is more than just coincidence because you'd sent the telepathic message to your friend who adjusted her actions to accommodate what she'd picked up from you before arriving at the restaurant.

As an intuitive, especially if you're clairaudient, you may telepathically pick up the thoughts of those around you. If you find that this ability is bothersome, you can use creative visualization to put a block up around your energy so that you're not continually picking up thoughts from others. Sometimes you will perceive the thoughts as complete sentences; other times, the thoughts are reflected as just general feelings that you'll get from the other person. You may also pick up a few words that relay the entire thought.

Out-of-Body Experiences

One phenomenon that many people have experienced is called the out-of-body experience (OBE). While there are many different religious and philosophical beliefs associated with an OBE, we're going to focus on the basics of what it is, how your intuitive abilities are associated with it, and how you can recognize and do this activity yourself.

While astral travel is considered to be an OBE, there are similarities and differences between the two. With astral travel, you're freely and intentionally choosing to visit and explore the astral plane. With an OBE, most people aren't intentionally trying to have an OBE, it just happens spontaneously. They may find it frightening and never want to have an experience like that again. Or they may be intrigued by the experience and want to learn more about developing their abilities in metaphysical topics. In both astral travel and an OBE, there is a silver cord connection from the astral body to the physical body, although in a spontaneous OBE the person may not be aware of the silver cord. In both instances, it is the astral body that leaves the physical body.

OBEs are usually short periods of time when a person is consciously aware of what is going on but they feel separated from their physical body. They often see their physical body from above and are aware of everything being said or done in the room around them. You usually hear about this type of OBE happening in hospitals when a person is ill, has had surgery, is experiencing some kind of trauma, or when they've been taking medications. Other times, the person may experience an OBE during times of normalcy, like when they are sleeping, dreaming, or just relaxing, and they can repeat conversations or describe events that really happened when they weren't physically there to experience them. Some people have even experienced OBEs when driving a car, or doing other tasks where their mind is relaxed. There isn't a specific criterion for when an OBE takes place; it can happen under any circumstances and at any time.

When you are intuitively in tune with your astral body, the chances of having an OBE increase. They may occur spontaneously at first, but with focus on intuitively connecting to your astral body, you can learn to separate from your physical body and have an OBE with your astral body staying in close proximity with your physical body. With practice, you can then learn to astral travel. In order to practice having an OBE, you will first tune into your ability of clairvoyance. Relax and focus on your astral body, then intuitively see it rise above your physical body. Try to look down and see your physical body below you. Then, move your astral body back down to your physical body and feel the two reconnect. Once you're comfortable doing this, you'll be ready to try moving into the astral plane.

Remote Injuries

Feeling pain in a specific part of your body, only to discover later that some-one you are close to has had an injury in exactly that same location, is an extreme form of empathy. Many people have this ability. In the past, I've had situations where I had such significant pain that came on suddenly that I actually went to the doctor, who was unable to find anything wrong with the area that hurt me. It wouldn't be until hours later that I discovered someone close to me had been injured in the same spot. Upon discovering the cause, my pain disappeared. At first I didn't understand why I would feel the same pain as someone else, but now I have a theory about why this happens.

When you're close to someone, you are able to connect intuitively with them through energy. It may be a spouse, child, sibling, parent, or friend. I find that this happens more often between people who are close than it does between strangers. That doesn't mean that as an intuitive you'll never pick up on a stranger's pain as a physical manifestation within your own body—you can. It's just more common between people who have some type of close relationship. The pain you feel may manifest in a number of ways. It may be the same type of pain as the injury itself, a pricking sensa-tion in the area of injury, or a shudder of pain that you feel move through your body at the moment the person is injured. You may also experience a feeling of unease during your day and an urgency to find out the cause of your pain. I'm not big on running to the doctor for every little thing, but in each instance where I've felt someone else's pain on a grand scale (because it was a major injury), I've found myself at the doctor's office within hours of the onset of pain.

It can be difficult to tell when the pain you're feeling is your own or someone else's. Sometimes there are subtle signs that will let you know the pain isn't yours; other times, you just have to deal with it until the true source has been revealed, especially if you've had yourself checked out and there wasn't anything wrong. If you do find yourself in this situation and nothing is wrong, sit quietly and focus your attention on whose energy you may be picking up. Once you feel you've connected to the correct person, call them up and make sure they're okay. If they aren't okay, you've discovered the root cause and your pain should dissipate quickly; if they are okay, then at least you'll have peace of mind where they're concerned and can try again to figure out where the pain coming from.

Energy and Electronics

You go through several cell phones a year; when your cell is working, it frequently drops calls or has static and other strange noises interfering with your conversation, especially when you're talking to someone who is also intuitive. You touch a light switch and the bulb blows, or you walk into a room and all the lights dim. Streetlights dim or blow when you're near. The electrical system, lights, or alternator in your car have problems. Your watch batteries drain much sooner than normal. Your computer frequently goes on the fritz and doesn't work the way it's supposed to—it loses its Internet connection, freezes, or has other problems that aren't related to technical difficulties or viruses. Does any of this sound familiar to you? These are all situations where your intuitive energy is affecting the electronics around you. It can be frustrating and expensive if you don't know how to control it.

People with abilities tend to have higher frequency levels and increased energy fields, which amplifies the electricity within them and can cause electrical malfunction. At other times, because intuitives use more energy, they pull it from the electronics around them, thus draining batteries or short-circuiting phones. The term "SLIDERS" (Street Lamp Interference Data Exchange) is often associated with people who have this ability. It's named after the street-light phenomenon in which people with this ability can not only make street lights turn on or off, but can affect any other electrical devices as well. For example, SLIDERS often can't wear watches for very long without them malfunctioning, regardless of the number of battery replacements made. They often have problems with static on cell phones, and dropped calls as well; they can have problems with the magnetic strips on credit cards malfunctioning after they've carried them on their person.

You may notice this happens more often when you're very excited, angry, or emotionally wound tight. Because the body is made up of electricity, people who have this ability are sent into overload when emotions run high. The electricity leaves your body and affects the electrical devices around you. People who have had encounters with electricity in the past are often affected more than others. In my case, I was nearly electrocuted as a child. You may have had a similar incident, had a near-death experience, or even been struck by lightning. Any major encounter with electricity can be a catalyst for this type of ability.

How do you control it so you're not spending a fortune on replacement electronics and light bulbs? One way you can control this ability is with white light. By putting a barrier of white light around you and giving it the intention of keeping you grounded and centered (even when your energy is running high), you can avoid shorting out devices around you. It doesn't always work, and sometimes you'll forget until you notice that electronics aren't acting normally around you. Just reinforce your barrier to stay grounded.

Electronics can also be affected by spirits, especially when they're trying to get your attention. Spirits blow light bulbs around me all of the time. If you have a barrier in place, but you're still experiencing difficulties with your electronics, take some time to sit quietly and ask the spirit or your guides if they have a message for you.

Driving

When you're driving, you are already in tune with your intuitive abilities as you watch the road. However, there are several things you can do that will help you avoid danger and arrive at your destination safely while keeping you centered and grounded. Though it's not always possible, you should always avoid driving when you're mad, upset, crying, or sleepy. As you get in your car, use creative visualization to see yourself reaching your destination safe and sound. Once inside, after you've safely buckled up, protect your car and its occupants with a bubble of white light. Next, take a moment to ground yourself by being aware of the wheels connecting to the road. Once you've done these things, begin driving. As you're driving, if you sense anything amiss in the energy fields around you, slow down, speed up, or stop as needed and as your intuition guides you. If you suddenly feel like you should go in an entirely different direction, then take an alternate course. How many times have you said, after the fact, "I should have taken that turn," or "if I'd only been five minutes earlier or later, this wouldn't have happened"?

Many people use driving time to think about the things going on in their lives. They may mull over situations, especially if they're having a problem with something, and arrive at a course of action or solution to a problem. You can also use driving time, when you're alone, to think about your intuitive abilities, to consider how they work for you, and to explore how you can enhance them. Driving isn't a time to do specific exercises because you should concentrate on the road, but it is a good time to give thought to your abilities. Thinking about them enables you to connect to them within you and that alone will allow you to grow in your abilities.

Lightning

During your life, as you develop your intuitive abilities, you will experience what I call "lightning." This type of lightning is spiritual, not the natural phenomenon that occurs during heavy storms, and it propels you along your path. It happens during times when your intuitive awareness increases dramatically and quickly, when you finally "click" with how your ability works, or any time that you experience an extreme jump in spiritual growth. You often experience this spiritual brand of lightning when you have moved from one level of understanding and enlightenment to the next.

Lightning feels like its name. It is a surge of energy that flows through you, increasing your inner light as it strengthens and empowers you. You can feel your frequency (your internal personal vibration) elevating, and you may suddenly understand new knowledge about your abilities, life path, or soul essence. Lightning affects all parts of you. It is a rejoining of your physical self to your spiritual self and everything in between, including your abilities and the way you think about the Universe. It can start at your core and blast outward to your extremities. Or it may feel as if it's coming through the top of your head at extreme speed, entering into your crown chakra, filling your body and spirit. Other times, it's a slow burn that builds from within your core essence until it's a hot fire scorching through you within minutes.

Lightning can also be a sign from your guides. They send it to you and are cheering beside you when you suddenly understand and accept a Universal Truth. Just as déjà vu allows you to know that you're on the right path, lightning wakes you and makes you aware and attentive so that you can experience even more spiritual growth. It is so powerful and electrifying that it can be life changing. You'll feel lighter and less stressed, and you will know that you are achieving what you set out to learn on the earthly plane.

When lightning happens, what's next? You keep on doing what you've been doing. You keep learning about your intuitive abilities and spiritual self. You learn more about the Universe and the Other Side. Then, when you least expect it, you'll experience lightning again. It can strike you many, many times during the course of your life. You may even come to expect it if you've gone through a period of growth. Don't be disappointed if it doesn't come when you think it will. It comes when you've mastered something on your life path, when you've grown and developed spiritually, when you've faced and embraced the intuitive and spiritual part of your soul. Lightning is part of your true essence, a reminder of who you are and where you're going in this lifetime.

Third Eye Information

Your third eye is related to the sixth sense and the sixth chakra, which is also called the third-eye chakra. It is located in the area between your eyebrows and your hairline, encompassing the forehead and going deep into the center of the brain at the pineal gland. It is thought to be in the center of the forehead or a little lower, right above the eyebrows. I tend to think of it as filling my entire forehead and sometimes it even feels like it encircles the top of my head and allows me to see both ahead of me and behind me. When you connect to your third eye, you'll feel its exact location within you. The third eye is important to your intuitive abilities because this is what you use to look at the energy patterns around you and on the Other Side, to view things while astral traveling and to look back on your physical body when you're having an OBE. Information from the third eye will sometimes feel as if it is coming in from one side or the other, from behind you or in front of you. As you learn more about your intuitive nature, each of these locations will have meaning to you.

Spirit guides usually show up on my right side and past life information on my left.

I'm specifically pointing out the third eye because it is so important when using your intuition. The third eye has no limits of space or time; you can see auras and other energy patterns using it, and it allows you to have visions. But how do you know if you've successfully opened your third eye? This is as unique to you as your hair color. Everyone will experience this differently. Some people have a process that they go through as the third eye is opening and they see a vision of it opening that may be symbolic to them. You may not experience it actually "opening" (I don't), but will know that it is open because you're using it. To keep it simple, you'll know when the third eye is open when you experience an intuitive event, which wouldn't be possible without your third eye being open. The following is an exercise you can do to try to open the third eye.

Try It Now: Connect with Your Third Eye

Here's what you do. Sit or lie down in a completely darkened room. Make sure there isn't any light coming in from streetlights or outside sources. Now, send your soul energy from the core of your being upward to the third eye. Use creative visualization to imagine it opening. Keep your physical eyes closed while you're looking into the darkness with your third eye. What do you see? If you have successfully opened your third eye, you will see a golden, white, or blue light. It can be soft and glowing or it can be bright and streamlined. It may illuminate the room so that you can see what's in it or you may only see the light within darkness. If you see any kind of light, then you have successfully opened your third eye.

Physical Manifestations of Intuitive Occurrences

Some intuitives are able to receive impressions as manifestations within their physical body. No, this is not possession. Sometimes an impression manifests as internal pain (see "Remote Injuries" earlier in this chapter); other times, it manifests in physical markings on the body. The intuitive may not realize what is happening at first, or give it any particular importance. Usually something that happens *after* the manifestation of the impression will bring you clarity about what happened.

Let me give you an example of this happening to me. My grandmother had heart problems and would get blackened, bruised-looking marks on her arms, the kind that go along with heart issues. One day a spot on the side of my wrist got really itchy and within moments a dark red, blood-blister-looking thing popped up on my skin. It was relatively big, about the size of a nickel, so my first thought was that something had bit me, but it happened while I was driving so I wasn't completely sure that it was a bug bite. It was a strange-looking mark, one that I haven't had since. I have a lot of dogs and horses so I thought that maybe I hit my wrist on something at the farm and didn't realize it, but I was pretty sure it hadn't been there before the itching started. Because I'm constantly getting scratched and bitten by things, which happens when you have animals, I didn't really think too much about it at the time. Two days later, my grandmother returned home to the Other Side. I was devastated, and it wasn't until that evening that I noticed the mark had completely disappeared as if I'd never had it at all. It was in that moment that I knew I had somehow received the mark as a sign of her impending death. I didn't get it at the time and I don't entirely know how it happened, but when it vanished from my skin right after her death, I knew it was somehow connected to her.

If you receive impressions in this way, then being in close proximity to a person with some sort of physical ailment may cause you to physically manifest symptoms of the other person—feeling pain in a part of your body only to discover they have pain or a problem in the same area, feeling hot when someone else has a fever, or physically feeling sick to your stomach when someone has a stomach virus—all of which disappear when you move away from the person. You usually will not have these physical symptoms as severely as the person that you're picking up on. This usually happens suddenly and you'll feel as if it doesn't belong to you. If you're sitting beside someone and suddenly start experiencing physical symptoms out of the blue, change your seat. If the symptoms go away, it is probably a physical manifestation of an intuitive impression you received from the person beside you.

Intuitives who experience their abilities in this way may notice that touching someone or something (see "Clairtangency/Psychometry" and "Try It Now: Psychometry" in chapter three) sets it off. Once you realize that this is a way that your abilities work, when it happens in the future you'll realize what is happening and can take appropriate action.

Karma

Karma is the idea that your actions from a past lifetime will have an effect, either positive or negative, in your current lifetime when you interact with souls whom you have previously known in a past life. The nature of the karma (positive or negative) is based on the intention behind your actions in that past life. In other words, what comes around goes around. For instance, if in a past life you intentionally treated someone badly, then in this lifetime you will have the opportunity to treat that same person in a kind manner to right the past wrong. Or, because you treated a person badly in a past lifetime, they may treat you badly in your current lifetime to balance your past actions.

When you consider that what you do will come back to you, in this lifetime or another, it becomes even more important to always base your actions in a place of love and positivity. That way, you will receive love and positivity in return. Treat others the way you want to be treated, and be aware that your intentions and actions will come back to you, one way or another and sooner or later.

There is also something called instant karma. Consider this event that I saw happen one day. A woman in a bad mood is checking out at the grocery store. She is rude to the cashier for no apparent reason other than she's in a bad mood herself and heatedly tells off the lady, who really hasn't done anything other than ring up her purchase and accept the payment. The woman grabs her bag of groceries, storms out the door, and runs right into the glass, knocking herself in the head because she tried to go out through an entry door, not the exit, and one that didn't open automatically. That's instant karma—the woman received a knock on the head for treating the cashier badly.

Overcoming Fears by Finding the Source in a Past Life

If you have a fear that you just can't seem to get a handle on, if your fear seems unreasonable even to you, or if you have an uncontrollable response to a specific thing, then it may be time to look to a past life for the instigating cause.

I've done many past life readings over the years and one question that I always ask before doing the reading is whether the person has any fears they can't get past. If they do, I'll look for the situation in the past life that caused this fear in the present. Most of the time, when a person connects with the original cause of said fear, they can understand and release it. Fear holds you back from reaching your fullest potential; therefore, it must be released so that you can proceed forward on your spiritual path. By finding the cause, the fear loses its hold over you and the negative fearful response is replaced by positive understanding.

Let's look at an example. In your past lifetime, you were a sailor. During one of your voyages, the ship sunk. You were below deck and were caught in a small room and couldn't get out, so you drowned in that lifetime. In your current lifetime, you're deathly afraid of the ocean and are severely claustrophobic. Remembering this past lifetime can help you release the fear of the ocean and the claustrophobia. Sometimes the effects are instant, but usually it takes time for you to completely let go of the fear so that you're no longer afraid at all. In this example, you may never love the ocean or small spaces, but you'll no longer be deathly afraid of them, either.

The Circle of Souls

Do you ever reincarnate with the same people that you knew in previous lifetimes? I think you do. As you move from one life to the next, you do so within the same circle of souls, even if you don't meet each of these souls in every lifetime. For instance, your mother from your past lifetime may be your son in your current lifetime or your son from the past is a coworker in this life. Your circle of souls is very large and layered. Those closest to you are in your inner circle in this lifetime but they may be in your outer circle in a future life.

If you've ever met someone and felt as if you'd known them forever, even though you'd just met, then you've encountered someone within your circle of souls. You've more than likely known this person very well in a past lifetime or over several lifetimes, and that is why they are so familiar to you now. It doesn't matter if they stay in your life for a short or long time during your current lifetime; it is the connection to them and to the past that allows you to bond with them on a soul level in the present.

Try It Now:
Connect with Your Circle of Souls

For this exercise you're going to make a list to connect to your circle of souls. Make enough columns on your paper to give each of the following groups its own column: your immediate family, your extended family, close friends, coworkers, and people from your past. You may need several sheets of paper to include all of the people you know. Now, once you've made the list, place stars beside the people with whom you've felt a close personal connection that resonates with you at a soul level. These are the people whom you have felt as if you've known before or whom you know so well that a large span of time could pass without you having contact with them and then, when you do reconnect, it feels as if you just saw them yesterday. These are the people in your circle of souls.

Once you have your list, take a few minutes and ask to see each person as they were when you met for the very first time. You're going to get past life information when you do this part. When they appear in your mind's eye, notice what they're wearing. Can you tell anything about the location from the background? If you see them wearing clothing that is no longer in use today, then that will give you an indication of the time. Notice as much as you can about what you're seeing because you are being shown the first lifetime that you lived with this person.

Test and Develop

Now that you've reviewed the types of psychic abilities, learned more about your own spirituality and intuitive nature, and determined your abilities, how do you develop your talents to their fullest potential? Where do you turn? What do you do?

The one thing that I would recommend above all else is to practice, practice, practice. Try to predict who is on the phone before you look at the caller ID or answer. When I was newly developing my abilities, one of my favorite ways to practice was to watch psychics on television and answer the audience members' questions before the psychic did. It doesn't count if you can't say it before the psychic speaks; if you think it but only say part of the answer, then you get half of a credit. It's a fun way to test your abilities and accuracy against the best and most famous in the metaphysical field. The more you use a talent, the better you become at it. That said, you should always trust in your own abilities because it may turn out that the person you're testing your abilities against might be wrong (no intuitive is 100 percent right) or tuning in to different information than you are; even worse, they might be a fraud.

Second on my list is to read everything you can get your hands on. There are so many excellent books on the market about intuitive abilities, the spirit realm, and metaphysics. There is a wealth of information at your fingertips; all you have to do is buy the book and begin your own reference library or check it out of the public library. Because we all experience our abilities in different ways, reading various experts' descriptions of a subject may enable you to find someone who experiences things in exactly the same way that you do.

Join online groups and then lurk. Sit back and read what people say but only take to heart what rings true to you. It's amazing how much you can absorb when someone else does the talking. Once you feel comfortable with the group, participate by asking questions and sharing your own experiences. I feel it is very important to share experiences because in that way others learn from you. Right now, you may be the one asking for advice and help as you hone your abilities. One day, someone may turn to you for advice. I'm a firm believer in what goes around comes around. We should all do our part to make sure what we're getting back is the best we can expect by giving our best now.

Once you've started feeling comfortable with your abilities, it's time to start pushing them. This is where you truly develop and expand. I think that we all go through several stages of developing our abilities. What I'd like to do now is explain these stages and offer ways for you to develop your abilities and reach the next level. For simplicity, let's just call these the beginning, intermediate, and advanced levels.

The Beginning Level: We've all been beginners at some point in our lives. This is completely normal. Regardless of the field, we all have to start at the beginning and learn. In the realm of metaphysics, this level is when you first realize that something is different with you. It's when you suddenly have the urge to search out more information about metaphysical topics and feel driven to do it from a spiritual level. It's when you pick up that first metaphysical book from the New Age section of the bookstore. Maybe you bought some runes or angel cards to go with that book on developing your intuitive abilities. At this stage, you may often correctly know who is on the phone when it rings, but you can't do it every time. Maybe you've felt a presence near you but weren't sure what it was. As you read and learned, you may have even started to include some metaphysical words in your vocabulary.

I like to compare these levels to a baby learning to walk. When you're a beginner in metaphysics, you're like the baby who can crawl. You've got the rocking down pat, can get up on all fours, and now you've got the movement going without falling flat on your face. This stage is not the time to start advertising your intuitive services to the world. This is still the time to research, study, and associate yourself with people who can mentor you.

How can you get to the intermediate level? When I was a beginner trying to expand my abilities, I used to practice with my best friend. She would test me by asking questions about someone before we saw them (for example, what color is so-and-so wearing to school today) and I would try to look for the answer. It was cool when I got it right. Practicing with a friend is one way to expand to the next level. Another way is to practice on your own. Try to make predictions about a variety of different situations. Or just sit quietly and listen to that voice that keeps trying to talk to you, which you may be ignoring. Your spirit guide just might have something very important to say to you.

Another good way is to open yourself to messages during meditation. Some people enjoy a formalized method of meditation. I personally don't have the time to use a formalized method because I have kids, animals, and businesses that require my attention. So I tend to like the "bathroom intuitive" approach. You're probably asking yourself what I mean by that, and I'll explain it in a moment. Quite often I get impressions when I'm in the bathroom, especially when I'm working on my own personal growth or trying to work out a personal problem. I could be in the shower or taking a bath when the impressions start coming through. Why is this? Because I'm letting my mind relax for a few minutes. I'm not focusing on anything except the hot water in the shower. When I first started thinking of the information I wanted to include in this book, Cassandra, my spirit guide, started giving me information while I was in the shower. I started laughing and asked her to please wait until I was some place where I could type it up or write it down.

The same thing happens regardless of the task at hand. We have horses, and mucking out their stalls takes a while because we have individual turn-outs attached to each stall. Let me tell you, picking up horse poop is boring work, but it's a great time to get impressions. It's amazing the kinds of information you can receive when you allow your thought processes to disengage and your mind to open up to the Universal Energy when doing mundane tasks.

The Intermediate Level: At this level, you've advanced far enough along your spiritual pathway that you've recognized that having abilities is only part of your overall growth. You've read and learned, and have mentors who are helping you to understand psychic abilities and spirituality. You now recognize that there is much more to learn and have claimed your growth and abilities as your own. Your selections at the bookstore may now include more specialized areas of metaphysics or paranormal topics because you're developing the areas that fit your path. You're feeling more comfortable with your inner self and the path you are taking. At this level not only are you still developing your abilities, but you're also expanding your consciousness to a higher plane.

You have moved past the beginning-level use of your abilities and are now concentrating your efforts on more individualized readings. At this level, you may be able to tap into a person's energy field to give them a reading; however, you may still be unsure and only relay information that is current and relevant to them without actually giving information that they can use. In other words, you're just telling them things they already know or that are too generalized to be specific to their needs. And that's totally fine. Everyone has to go through these types of readings in order to move into deeper parts of a person's energy.

To get to the advanced level, you not only have to trust your guides and yourself, but you must also make a concentrated effort to focus on raising your frequency (your personal vibrational level) by accepting that this is your path and allowing yourself to absorb all that you are offered. It's very easy to get stuck in the intermediate level because you are at a place of comfort. To get to the advanced level, you must take that step outside your comfort zone, take a leap of faith, and dive headfirst into your spiritual path. It's not an easy thing to do, but once you take that step, the rewards far outweigh any fears you may have had.

The Advanced Level: At this level you're still learning. In fact, you'll continue to learn new things about metaphysical topics throughout your entire life. You've come a long way since your days as a beginner. You've probably taken a few years to get to this level (I know for me it took over twenty, but then again, I didn't get here willingly but fought it most of the way). You now have a greater understanding of your spiritual self, your role in the Universe, and your relationship with your spirit guides; and if you want to, you're able to give in-depth, detailed readings. You could, if you so desired, become a spiritual coach, which entails so much more than just doing readings. You could also be a mentor or a public speaker. It is up to you to decide how far you want to share yourself with others to aid in their enlightenment.

At this level, you are able to tap into the Universe's higher energy. You are able to connect directly to the energy fields of those you read. You may still use runes, tarot cards, crystals, or other tools associated with divination, but you don't necessarily need them. When you use these tools, you'll lay out the cards, runes, or crystals, but you're connecting on a much higher level than these tools can give you. Some people will seek you out specifically for these types of readings, so the tools still have their worth if you choose to use them. For example, when I'm unclear about an aspect of a reading or if I'm getting conflicting impressions, I will sometimes draw one oracle card to clarify.

Since the advanced level is the highest that we can attain, how can you make yourself even stronger and grow further along your path? By becoming a spiritual coach, acting as a mentor, and sharing your insights with others, you are not only helping them move along their own spiritual path but you're also moving further along yours.

In order to accept your abilities, you must first realize how they connect to your physical self and your soul essence in this lifetime. If you are an empath, you will feel other's emotions, but how can you separate those emotions from your own? If you're clairvoyant, how do you physically know when you're getting an impression? What is different physically that lets you know that an experience is indeed an intuitive impression? This is key in understanding how your abilities work. Can you find a source for the emotion? Do you feel like you're in a semi-trance when you get a clairvoyant message? How can you connect the source to yourself? Once you learn to differentiate between your own feelings and emotions and information that is given to you from an outside source, you're well on your way along your spiritual path.

Intense emotions heighten your intuition—at least that's my experience. Once you open the door and recognize your abilities, you're able to do more and more. Your understanding will increase through experience. You'll be better at some things than others; some of you will excel as clairvoyants, others as aura readers, and still others at palmistry, and so on. Find the path that calls to you and follow it, and you will excel.

As with any type of study, if you think you have abilities in any of these areas, do more research. Read as much as you can on the topic and take what you feel applies to you and what will be helpful at this point of your development. As I have said before, my point of view is only one of many. If something doesn't make sense, or you feel it doesn't apply to you, then pass it by. At a later date you may feel differently, but you should always follow what you feel is right in your heart. Each of us has our own truths that are in continual growth and development. You'll know it when you connect with yours.

Regardless of what level you are currently on as you test and develop your intuitive abilities and progress along your spiritual path, always lead from the heart. Let love guide you, let trust edge you forward, and always treat others with the respect that they deserve. Be honest with yourself, don't be overconfident, and keep your humility. If you can do these things, then you truly will become all that you can be, all that you've charted and planned to learn through your life lessons.

....

Now that you've discovered some of the ways that you can have psychic experiences, talk with your friends to see if they, too, have had any of these things happen to them. You're not alone on this path. In fact, many, many people have similar experiences. More and more people are opening up about psychic abilities and are willing to discuss them. The topic isn't as taboo as it used to be. There are people who can help you, mentor you, and assist you on your path of enlightenment if you need or want help along the way. All you have to do is seek them out.

Seven

Types of Readers/
Readings/Spirit Beings

Do you know how many different types of intuitive readings there are? Divination itself has hundreds of different methods. You can learn many more than what I've discussed in the scope of this book. Let's take a look at some of the different types of readings that you can receive or give, or do simply for yourself.

Spirits are all around us. You may not recognize them at first, or you may choose to ignore them simply because you're not ready to receive their assistance, but they are there just the same. When the time is right, you will learn to connect with your guides or to recognize others in the spirit world. Some of the greatest moments of enlightenment I've ever had were through my spirit guides. I wish the same for you. In this chapter, we'll look at the different kinds of spirits and ways they can make themselves known to you; we'll also look at the different types of readings and the people who do them.

Most, if not all, of the intuitives and readers discussed in this chapter use the clair abilities. As you examine the types of readers, consider whether you, too, should be included in this category based on your intuitive abilities, or whether you could become one of these readers if you continue to develop your abilities. There are many ways that you can use your abilities. Do you have an ability that is unique? If so, you may be able to fill a niche and help others along their path while using that ability. You are already an intuitive; it's up to you to decide how you will use the ability. Take the time to consider your path and your desires when it comes to developing your intuitive nature. This is a lifelong process that can't be rushed.

Akashic Records/Readers

The Akashic Records are interactive books that contain a recording of every soul's journey from the beginning of time. Contained within the Akashic Records are every thought, emotion, word, action, missed opportunity, desire, lesson, variance of personal frequency, decision, and nuance of every soul's spiritual journey. The Hall of Records, where the Akashic Records reside, is an unlimited space of pure energy. The Akashic Records show our connections to other souls and animals and include details all of our lifetimes, as well as the lessons learned and the lessons we're still working on. The Akashic Records contain our life maps for each incarnation, and it is where we can go to see if we're indeed on the right track.

Think of the records as a library with books for each lifetime of every soul. For those who can access the Akashic Records, it is a phenomenal resource for spiritual growth and development. The Akashic Records can reveal your soul truths and your spiritual path.

An Akashic Record reader is an intuitive who is able to access the records on the Other Side to obtain and deliver information for the person whom they are reading. We all have access to the Akashic Records; it's just a matter of knowing how to get to them and how to read them. During an Akashic Record reading, the intuitive will access your records. Each intuitive has different methods of how they retrieve the records and the method I share here is based on my own experience.

I had been doing Akashic Record readings for years before I ran across a name to describe the place I was accessing, which is an indicator that you have to follow your own path and understand your own intuitive nature in order to grow. Because, when I did learn what it was, it was a huge confirmation of the work that I do. I had to experience it firsthand and then later find out that other people experienced it in the same way as I did and had used the same terminology to describe it. That was one of those moments where I experienced the Chills of Universal Truth.

I called the place where I received my information during a reading the "Hall of Records," and I still refer to it that way most of the time. In order to get to the Hall of Records, I clear my energy of any negativity that I may have accumulated during the day, then I envision myself moving through the layers of the Other Side until I am in a place of high frequency and positively charged light. Then the Hall of Records appears directly in front of me as a huge set of stairs with large fluted columns that are at least twelve feet wide, all made of shiny white marble. The columns are massive and as I look upward at them, I can see the beginnings of decoration at the top but I can't see where the column ends. I climb the steps thinking about the person I'm there to read for and wait until the man I call the "Gatekeeper," the "Guardian," or the "Guardian Gatekeeper" shows up. His appearance is that of an old man; he has a long white beard and white hair that reaches his shoulders. He's dressed differently every time I see him. He hands me the book that contains the information that I need. In my experience, he is the sole entity that can go into the Hall of Records and get the books. Everyone can access the material but only he can give you the correct book, at least in my experience; yours may be different.

The books also appear to me in a variety of forms. They may have hard, flat covers or puffy ones. Most seem to have some sort of decoration on the cover that is symbolic of your life path. I've seen jewels, golden stitching, and a number of different designs on the book cover. Then, holding the book between my palms with the outer edge of the pages pointing upward, I open the book and let the pages flutter down, opening the book to the passage I'm supposed to read. I read the information, normally typing as I read, and that is what I deliver to the person I'm reading for. Sometimes I am given more than one book to read during the session and sometimes it's already opened to a specific page when it's handed to me. When it's over, I thank the Guardian Gatekeeper for allowing me to read the passage(s) and then he'll go on his way and I walk back down the steps as I leave my trancelike state. You, too, can access the Akashic Records in this way. When you visit, just be clear in your intent and the reason you need to check the records.

Psychics/Intuitives/Spiritual Consultants/Mediums

A psychic is a person who uses any of the clair abilities (see chapter three) to do a reading for another person in order to answer specific questions about present situations or future occurrences.

Every person is born with intuitive (psychic) abilities. Some choose to develop their abilities and use them to help others along their spiritual path while others only use their abilities for themselves. Some people deny their abilities and others embrace them. Whatever scenario fits you, it's the right one for you in this lifetime and on your spiritual path. You may have had situations where you felt that you were tapping into your intuitive nature but were unsure. If this is the case, you can always choose to explore your abilities further and learn to use them.

During a reading, an intuitive (psychic) will tell you what they see for you at the time of the reading. However, this can change based upon the decisions you make between the time of the reading and the event occurring. You can even prevent things from happening with your decisions. Just as each of us has abilities, each of us also has free will. It is this free will that gives us the choice to allow or to avoid the things seen during the reading. Each person who does readings approaches it differently. This is because each person is a unique individual. The way I do a reading and the way you do a reading may be completely different in method and procedure, but we may pick up similar information.

Using their abilities, a spiritual consultant—whether they call themselves an advisor, counselor, or coach—helps a person connect with themselves at a soul level through intuitive readings. This allows the person to understand their spiritual nature through the development of their own abilities. A spiritual consultant may offer a variety of spiritual readings such as accessing the Akashic Records, revealing past lives, mentoring, or angel and spirit guide communication. These types of readings address the growth that is needed to progress along a person's spiritual path; they help a person understand and connect to their soul essence and see themselves as a spiritual being. Spiritual consultants may also offer a variety of intuitive readings as well. Some readings may use tools such as cards or runes, or they may just be done using intuition or clair abilities. These readings will answer specific questions for the person, and these answers might enable them to understand current situations. With this gained clarity, they are better equipped to handle situations in their lives, allowing for more spiritual growth.

Spiritual consultants should never tell a person what to do or what actions to take. The decision must always come from within the person getting the reading, from the core of their soul's essence. The intuitive coach can give the information that they see, but it is up to the person receiving the reading to process that information, make their own decisions, and grow in their own spirituality.

The term "psychic medium" is relatively new and there is still some confusion as to exactly what a psychic medium is and what they can do. While all mediums have psychic ability, not all psychics are mediums because they may not be contacting entities in the spiritual realm to gain their insight. A psychic medium is a person who has one or more psychic abilities as well as the ability of *mediumship*, which is communicating with those who have returned home to, or reside on, the Other Side. Mediums also have the ability to communicate directly with spirit guides, masters, and angels. Because there are a lot of misunderstandings when it comes to psychic mediums, I want to clarify what I believe a psychic medium can and cannot do.

A psychic medium will tell you that they cannot "summon" the dead. Instead, when doing a reading for you, they will tell you who they see or sense around you and then deliver any messages that spirit may choose share with them (if any). They will not guarantee that they can connect with the specific departed loved one you want to contact. Why? Because who shows up in spirit form is completely out of the psychic medium's control. To promise contact when you can't guarantee delivery is simply playing on the emotions of the person left behind, which is unethical. During a reading you may want to talk to your favorite uncle but instead the aunt that grated on your nerves is the one who appears. She may have a message for you that will enable you to understand your relationship with her, a message that gives you peace or helps you deal with a situation in your life. I firmly believe that a spirit isn't going to show up unless there's a specific reason they need to communicate with you.

When a psychic medium makes contact, they do it in a number of ways. Mediums quite often see a physical representation of the spirit and can describe what they're wearing and their physical appearance. Other mediums do not see a physical manifestation of someone standing in front of them but instead see a spirit manifested in their third eye. They may clairvoyantly see the spirit before them, hear them talk through clairaudience, see them through their third eye, consciously or unconsciously channel the spirit, or use telepathy. Psychic mediums may do group readings, or séances, and usually do not use divination tools during the mediumistic part of a reading. For instance, if I'm right in the middle of a clairvoyant reading and a spirit pops in with a message, I stop what I'm doing and attend to the spirit message. When it's over, I'll go back to the clairvoyant reading.

Before getting a reading with a psychic medium, you should check them out, and find out how they conduct their readings, then get the reading with them if you feel a connection with them and agree with the way they work. You may discover that some mediums will say they're not psychics and that only a medium can deliver messages from the Other Side. While the "medium" part is true, these mediums are just not using the term "psychic" because they prefer the word "medium". Quite honestly, the word "psychic" has gotten a really bad reputation due to the sheer number of unethical people calling themselves psychics who haven't properly honed and practiced their abilities, so it's no wonder that people with true, trained abilities are turning away from the word. Others, myself included, prefer the word "intuitive" to describe their abilities. Without the ability of mediumship and the clair abilities, psychic mediums wouldn't be able to communicate with spirits, just as someone who is very psychic but who lacks the ability of mediumship will not be able to deliver messages to you from beyond.

Psychic Detectives

A psychic detective is normally thought of as someone who uses their intuitive abilities to help law enforcement officers solve crimes. Most people who do this are at high spiritual frequencies and have been working as a professional intuitive for many years. Some police departments never accept the help of psychics and others are more open to receiving assistance in this manner. When psychics are used by the law, it's normally kept under wraps and psychic detectives are often only called in as a last resort.

Psychic detectives work on many different kinds of cases—robberies, missing persons, cold cases, and the like. They can often give a different perspective on the crime, and the information received by the intuitive may point the police in a different direction where they may discover new clues.

Not all psychic detectives work with the police, nor do they own a detective agency. You're a psychic detective if you've ever used your intuitive abilities to obtain information that you've needed, or to find a lost item that belongs to you or another person, if you've intuitively scanned someone who made you feel uncomfortable or scared, or if you've used remote viewing to check on a loved one. These are all forms of psychic detective work.

You may also use your psychic detective abilities in paranormal investigations. Many psychic detectives regularly assist local paranormal investigative units in this way. Paranormal investigators want to see if a psychic detective's impressions are in sync with what they are picking up at the site. Whether you choose to use your abilities to find a lost object, help the police track down a criminal, or aid paranormal investigators, you can be a psychic detective if that is where your path is leading you.

Medical Intuitives

Before we get into what a medical intuitive is and what they can do, I need to say that information received from a medical intuitive should never be used as a replacement for proper medical treatment. If you choose to use the services of a medical intuitive, use their readings along with the treatment deemed necessary by a licensed medical doctor. Medical intuitives are not doctors and cannot in any way diagnose or treat disease of any kind. That being said, there are many medical doctors who are also medical intuitives who *can* diagnose and treat disease. There are also people who could be classified as medical intuitives but shy away from the term because they do not have the proper medical licensing and credentials behind their name, therefore they will not offer medical impressions.

If you have ever known a person's medical problem by reading their energy or aura, then you have the ability to be a medical intuitive. Medical intuitives are people with a highly developed sense of intuition who specifically look for and obtain information about the internal workings of the human body through analyzing the energy held within that body, thereby identifying potential problems before they become dysfunctional and turn into an illness. Medical intuitives can read information about any of the complex systems within human anatomy by intuitively scanning for areas that are out of balance. Some medical intuitives see problems within the body as dark gray or black spots, holes, fading or blurred sections, or other types of disturbances within the energy field. When found early, these areas of imbalance can be brought into balance before the onset of disease or severe medical problems. Medical intuitives can do this for both medical illnesses and emotional issues that require further attention by a licensed medical professional.

For true healing to occur, any emotional issues that block the natural flow of your frequency must be addressed in addition to receiving medical treatment. If you're holding on to fear, it has to be released. As a medical intuitive, you can also look inside yourself, find those emotions you're hanging on to, address them, and bring about inner healing.

My dad has always said this about illness: "If you think about it hard and long enough, it'll happen. If you're in stressful situations over a long or extended period of time, you'll get bellyaches and headaches. If you worry over it long enough, it'll do something to you and make you sick." But he also believes that this applies to alleviating illness as well. I remember a story that he told me about a wart that he had on his elbow. Every time he looked at it, he said to himself, that's getting smaller. Pretty soon, the wart was gone. So you see, your emotional frame of mind can positively or negatively affect your physical body. If you're the kind of person who holds your emotions inside, never releasing them, then you may be causing issues that would disappear if you'd just fly off the handle every once in a while.

Spirit Guides/Ancestral Guides/Departed Spirits

What is a spirit guide? The words are pretty easy to understand—it's a spirit that guides. A *spirit guide* is a soul on the Other Side who has agreed to help us move along our path toward greater spiritual growth and enlightenment while we are residing on the earthly plane. They watch over us from the Other Side. Spirit guides have an extremely high vibrational rate; they teach us and help us learn our life lessons.

Does everyone have a spirit guide? I believe that each of us has many guides over our lifetime. I've found that we have one or two who are our life guides, meaning that they have been with us since birth and are always there to help us with anything and everything that we experience. Then we have other guides who are with us for shorter periods of time to help us with specific lessons or during times of need. One guide may help raise your vibrational level, another one may help you deal with a family crisis, and another one helps you learn lessons of trust. Spirit guides have very positive energy and only have your best interests at heart. Everyone has spirit guides just as everyone has guardian angels, though the two are not the same. If you're intuitively aware, you can make contact with these highly developed spiritual entities. Sometimes first contact can be difficult, but your spirit guide will never give up trying to get through to you.

How do you communicate with your guides? Usually the messages received are related to your current lifetime and are received telepathically. You'll get a feeling that you act on, or you'll have a thought that makes you pay attention to a certain detail or event. They can come to you in dreams to deliver messages that you may be ignoring during your waking hours. It's easy to become distracted with the stresses of daily life and not pay attention to the communications your guides are trying to give you. When this happens, then they may have better success at reaching you during dreams. Or they may help you by creating syn-chronicities that really grab your attention and make you more aware. In other words, if you won't listen to the subtle messages, they'll knock you over the head with it. Spirit guides may also be connected to you from past lifetimes, so they show you things from that past lifetime to help you understand the present—but this can be confusing if you don't remember the past lifetime.

The easiest way that I have found to connect to my guides is to sit quietly, put a protective bubble of white light around myself, ask that only higher level entities are allowed to contact me, clear my mind, and then reach out telepathically to my guides. I ask them to connect with me and deliver any messages that I should know at this point on my life path. My guides often visit my dreams, because as they say, I'm thickheaded and don't pay enough attention, and it's easier to connect that way. What can I say? I have a lot of things going on in my life that distract me, but I always come back around.

When you're connecting with your guides, it's very rare that they will be someone famous whom you've heard of in your current lifetime. Your guides may or may not have previously incarnated. They can appear in any form. I've seen guides fully dressed in period clothing, in white garb, as a ball of golden energy, as an animal totem, and as male or female. Guides tend to give you messages that will enable your spiritual growth instead of predicting future events in your life. You have free will and they normally don't predict outcomes, but will instead guide you on your life path. If you're experiencing difficulties connecting with your guides, sometimes you'll be successful if you speak your questions out loud. Write down your experiences with your guides in your journal so that you can refer back to them. While some events will be so profound that you'll never forget them, the everyday encounters may tend to fade in your memory. Writing them down allows you to refer back to them at a later date. When reaching out to your guides, open your intuitive channels and remain receptive to the spirit guides who choose to contact you.

Here's a scenario for you. Say you're in the middle of planning a big event. You are suddenly presented with a problem that must be solved immediately, but you can't make that decision based on the circumstances involved. Suddenly, you come up with an alternate resolution that you'd never considered before that will solve the problem without adversely affecting the rest of the event. Is this your spirit guide or your imagination? It very well could be your mind just giving you an alternative, but if the information feels like it's coming from outside of you, then it's more likely that you're being guided by someone from the Other Side. Many times in life you may have a flash of knowledge that, when you really think about it and examine how the information was received, will feel as if it came from outside of you. When this happens, it is often your spirit guides leading the way.

An *ancestral guide* is a spirit guide who has incarnated within your family heritage at some point and thus shares a blood relationship with you. As the name suggests, they are your ancestors, your relatives. It is their role to watch over the lineage and to heal and help resolve family disputes. They may be a father, mother, grandmother, grandfather, aunt, uncle, sister, brother, or even your great-great-great-great-great-great-great-great-great-grandmother. Ancestral guides appear in your life when you need them and it's always by their choice, not yours, when they show up. They often appear when least expected, when you're trying to solve a specific problem, when you're emotionally in need, or when they just want you to recognize that they are around to support you. You may or may not recognize them, depending upon when they were alive in your family.

Ancestral guides communicate with you in the same ways that your spirit guides contact you. They may appear in your third eye, visions, or dreams. They may send you messages through music, smells, words, or symbols that bring their memory to mind. Love is the reason that ancestral guides will visit you. They are your family and their presence is a way to let you know that love lives forever. Sometimes they'll be with you for a short while as you handle a specific situation and other times they appear quite often. When someone passes from your life to the Other Side, they may still watch over you and try to communicate with you, or they may prepare to reincarnate again. If you have developed your mediumistic ability, you will be able to receive messages that the deceased have for you. If you're not a medium, you can still receive signs that a spirit sends through your intuition. You'll know in your gut (feel instinctually) that what just happened is a message from someone on the Other Side.

What types of signs can spirits give you? Most often they will try to communicate in subtle ways. You may discover that the picture of them on the mantle has been moved or laid down, or a photo on the wall is tilted after you just straightened it. They also can project smells that you would associate with them. For instance, if your uncle always smoked a cigar, or your aunt wore a rose perfume, or if your mom always smelled like baking, it is likely that the occurrence of these scents in places where there isn't a source for them is your ancestral guide telling you they are close by. In my own experience I've had spirits get really creative. I've had loved ones that have passed shock me out of a crying spell over them by visually appearing in my third eye, shaking their finger at me and saying, "Stop that crying right now!" I've had them hug me to let me know everything is okay and that they're with me, and I've had them move things to an impossible location where I had to search and search to find something I was using just moments before, just to let their presence be known. They can also leave items that you would associate with them in impossible places.

When people pass, you may desperately want to contact them or have them contact you. Sometimes, spirits may not come around right away because emotions are still too raw or because they're busy on the Other Side. If they choose to come back, when the time is right you'll be able to sense them if you're open to their presence. When you open your abilities and mindset to the possibilities of life after death, you also open yourself to the joy of connecting with your loved ones after they have passed.

Elemental and Nature Spirits

Throughout the ages, people have reported experiencing contact with elemental spirits, also called nature spirits, which take the form of fairies, elves, leprechauns, gnomes, and sprites to name a few. Many intuitives also have the ability to communicate directly with these entities that live in and help nature. Some elemental spirits can also act as guides. There are many different beliefs about nature spirits and elementals, so I'll just tell you my take on them from my personal experience.

My first contact with a nature spirit was when I was told by a spirit that I was "coming into" my natural abilities and that I would get really sick, but afterward I would know things. It happened exactly as I was told and many years later, during a group medium session, this same nature spirit gave me his name, Robert, and reminded me of that first encounter. At that time I hadn't told anyone about that experience, so there was no way for the medium or anyone else in attendance to have such detailed prior knowledge of exactly what happened that day. During the session, I noticed sparkles of light flitting about the room, often near the ceiling, and found out afterward it was the manifestation of the spirits in attendance. It was the first time I'd seen that happen, but not the last. If you think a nature spirit is nearby, allow your eyes to go a bit out of focus as you look around. Sometimes it makes them easier to see.

The movie industry often depicts nature spirits as evil, but I disagree with this portrayal. I believe that their purpose is to care for the earth. They are extremely wise, nonjudgmental conscious beings. Since my experience with a nature spirit, I also believe that they help people on their life paths just as guides do. Guides take a more active role than nature spirits as we progress on our life path, but if you're in tune with your nature spirits, they can be of great assistance by helping you have moments of inspiration or insight, bringing harmony into your life, and helping clear negativity.

Nature spirits can also help you find things that you've lost if you'll only ask them. This is especially true of small things like a button that has popped off of your shirt, an earring, ring, or other hard-to-find article. Once I lost the back to my earring in a deep plush carpet. I searched and searched and finally I asked my nature spirits to help me find it. A while later, I found it sitting on my dresser in plain view, when I know for a fact it hadn't been there moments earlier and that no one in my household had entered my room and put it there. Nature spirits are always around when you're outside, so the next time you're on a bike ride in the park or are working outside, ask them to give you a sign of their existence.

Spirit Messengers

Spirit messengers can come in many different forms. A spirit messenger may be an animal that shows up at a particular time just to stare at you; when you notice the animal, pay attention to what is going on within you in that particular moment and you'll often realize an important lesson. When you grasp the message, the animal usually leaves. Spirit messengers can also come in the form of a person who walks up to you and says something very profound, which leaves you stunned and enlightened, and then walks away and seems just to vanish, which also makes an impact because you know the person couldn't have just disappeared like that.

These messengers come at very specific times in order to make you recognize a moment in your life. When it happens, it may seem odd enough that you become very drawn into that moment and will likely never forget it. This moment may be confirmation that you are on the right path, or it may be an epiphany or turning point in your life. Take a minute right now to think about when a spirit messenger came into your life to make you notice a moment.

Shadow People

You see them in your peripheral vision at any time during the day or night—the dark, shadowy, human forms. They lack specific features, like a face, and sometimes appear only as mist. They may be wearing a hooded cloak or a hat and may have golden or red eyes, or they may even have a colored glow to them like gold, blue, or purple. You notice them as a darting movement out of the corner of your eye, or you are overwhelmed with the uneasy feeling that someone is watching you until you notice them standing right in front of you. At first you may think it was just your imagination playing tricks on you, and if you tell someone who has never experienced this phenomenon, they'll likely agree. But when you see this unexplainable occurrence, these dark forms, multiple times and on different occasions, the imagination theory goes out the window because you believe what you saw and start searching for answers. What are these manifestations and why are you seeing them?

There are many theories about the shadow people phenomenon. While I can't rule out any possibility since we really don't know what these forms are yet, and because I work with energy, vibrations, and frequency, I believe you are intuitively seeing into another dimension or energy field and are picking up the movement of beings within these dimensional energy fields. Some of the other theories are that they are ghosts in shadow form, demons or evil entities, time travelers, the astral bodies of people having OBEs while astral traveling, or protective spirits. These entities never seem do to anything but observe our actions, and often appear to flee when noticed.

While no one can say for sure what these manifestations truly are, one thing is for certain: it's your clairvoyant ability that allows you to see them and your empathic ability that enables you to feel their presence.

Trance Channel/Conscious Channel/Channeling

What does it mean when an intuitive says that they "channel" spirits? Channeling is done by a psychic medium (someone who has the ability to connect to departed loved ones, spirit guides, or other entities on the Other Side). They act as a vessel for those who want to communicate messages from the spirit realm to someone in the physical realm. This can be done by speaking the message, writing it down, or typing it in a document or e-mail.

Channeling almost always happens in an altered state, but there are different levels of alteration. Because a medium is the vessel for information to come through, you (the medium) will usually forget the details soon after the reading in any type of channeling session. The information can come through a light or deep trance channel or a conscious channel. Regardless of how the message is received by the medium, you'll usually discover that it is full of important information. The messages can seem prophetic, down-to-earth, wise, enlightening, and conversational, as if your best friend is talking to you. A channeled message is often received in person, via e-mail, or even sometimes over the phone. If you've never seen a deep trance channel work in person, it's a very enlightening experience.

There are primarily four different types of ways mediums engage in channeling. Let's take a look at each one.

Fully Conscious Channel: When you're engaged in a fully conscious channel, you're using your intuitive abilities to connect to a spirit who wants to deliver a message to someone else. You feel completely normal, are fully awake, and can start and stop the channeling session if you're interrupted. You remember the entire channeling session with clarity for a short while after it's over and may remember parts of it for a much longer time, especially if the information affected you as the intuitive. Sometimes information that comes through can help the intuitive as much as it helps the person they're reading.

Altered-State Conscious Channel: This is when you think you are fully conscious during the channeling session, but afterward you realize that you were in more of a heightened state of awareness and were focusing differently than you do when you are fully conscious. You may remember some details of the channeling session but not with the same level of clarity that you experience when you're doing a fully conscious channeling session.

Light Trance Channel: This is when you're channeling while in a light trance. During the trance you may feel a bit displaced but you're still the one receiving and delivering the message where it needs to go. You're still within your body; you've just allowed your mind to go out of focus so that you can connect to the spirit you're trying to communicate with on the Other Side. They best way to describe how this feels is to compare it to the way you feel during a daydream.

Deep Trance Channel: This is when you're channeling while in a deep trance. Your being is displaced and you allow another being, spirit, or entity to occupy your body in order to deliver information or messages directly to someone else, using your body and voice as the conduit. Depending on the abilities of the person in the deep trance, they may or may not remember the channeling session. There are some excellent and inspiring books based on information received during deep trance channeling. This method isn't for everyone, though.

It doesn't matter which of these methods you use; you just have to make sure that the one you choose is right for you and that you feel comfortable doing it. You may use one or you may use all four, depending upon the situation. Try these various ways of channeling to discover the one that fits you the best.

Try It Now: Channeling in a Light Trance

To do this exercise, you're going to sit at your computer keyboard with a blank document open. If you don't have a computer, sit with a notebook and ink pen. Protect yourself with white light and put yourself into a light trance by "zoning out" as if you're daydreaming. Ask your guides to give you some information that will be beneficial to you in your life. Then type up or write the information that you receive either through a vision, hearing spoken words, or just "knowing" the information. Bring yourself out of the slight trance by refocusing on being "in the now." Read what you have typed or written from your guides. You may notice that it is in a different tone of voice than how you normally speak or write. Determine how the information is beneficial to you at this time. Make sure that you thank your guides for their assistance.

Angel Readers/Angel Communication/ Guardian Angels

Angels are beings of light who aid us in times of need. Angels are not the same as your spirit guides; they reside on a different dimension of the Other Side. Just as we each have spirit guides who are with us for our entire lifetimes, we also have guardian angels who are with us for our entire existence on earth.

To receive help from your angels, you have to ask them to assist you. While a spirit guide will try to reach out to you, angels will not interfere or reach out unless you are in a desperate circumstance or if you have asked for their help. Once you have been touched by an angel, especially if they've saved your life, you'll never erase that event from your memory. My husband was in a near-fatal car wreck where he died on the scene and was brought back to life. He was in the hospital for quite a while, and because I didn't have anyone to watch my son, I had to stay at my parents' house an hour and a half away. I'd leave the house at five every morning and drive to the hospital so I could be with my husband while my mom watched my son. One morning as I was nearing a curve, I was overwhelmed with the scent of lilacs, roses, wisteria, and lavender all mixed up together and I heard a shout saying "STOP!" I immediately slammed on the brakes, thinking that a wild animal was going to jump out in front of me. But as I went around the curve at about twenty miles per hour, I saw a car's taillights as it backed out into the road, right in my direct pathway. If my angel hadn't interfered that day, who knows what would have happened to me? Thank you, angel.

Intuitively connecting with your angels will help you to live a more spiritual life. Angels can bring peace and happiness and enable you to live life to your fullest potential spiritually—if you sincerely want their help. They can assist you in developing your abilities so that you can fulfill your spiritual quests. All you have to do is ask.

Angels can also manifest to you in human form, especially if you've asked for their help and then don't listen to their guidance. They may just walk up to you in the grocery store, retail store, or while you're sitting on a park bench enjoying nature. They start up a conversation or just deliver a message and then disappear. The disappearing part, I believe, is so that we know that we've just had a spiritual encounter, because we know for a fact that there is no way—in the amount of time elapsed and the distance that we can view—that a flesh-and-blood person could have vanished into thin air. An angel can. When you call on your angels, make sure you remain intuitively open to them so that you can receive and understand the help they're giving at your request.

Angels are messenger beings who have never incarnated in the earthly realm. They are celestial beings with highly elevated frequencies. From your personal angels to the archangels, they are waiting to help you whenever you trust in them, open your heart, and call on them for assistance. Knowing and communicating with your angels allows you to connect with your own divinity.

Angel readers are mediums who can specifically connect to your angels, who are with you at all times. Getting an angel reading is a positive experience that helps you to connect to and receive loving guidance from your angels. Angel readers should be able to tell you whether your angels have a male, female, or androgynous energy; each angel's name; how long they have been with you (as in how many lifetimes); and why they are with you (what life lessons they're helping you with, if you give them permission to share that information). They can deliver any messages that the angels have for you.

It is comforting to know that your angels are with you at all times, ready to assist you in all that you do if you only ask them. If you're curious as to how many angels you have, an angel reader will be able to help you meet them; some angel readers may even teach you to directly connect to your angels. Meeting your angels in this manner can empower you, give you the strength to deal with hard situations in your life, and enable you to make long-term plans through goal setting. Knowing your angels will help you grow as they guide you along your spiritual journey.

Aura Reading/Aura Balancing

The *aura* is the electromagnetic energy field that emanates from people and objects. An aura reading is when an intuitive has the ability to see these energy fields around living beings and can receive impressions about a person from this energy. When reading a person's aura, the first thing that comes to mind is glowing colors that extend from the person's physical body. These fields may appear as white to a beginner and as radiant, color-filled energy to those who are more advanced at reading auras. I tried for years to see auras surrounding a person's body, but I just couldn't do it. All I'd ever see was a white glowing light around their edges, usually at school when my teachers wrote on the blackboard, and never any other color. If I looked with my third eye, I could see the energy clearly and the colors associated with it, but it was in the wrong place. I finally realized that when I did energy readings I was actually seeing and reading from the person's aura, but not in the place or way that it's typically done. For me, auras are a river of energy that goes around the person's waist, flowing from the right elbow around to the left and then behind them back to the right. I will usually see colors in this energy as well as the depth of the energy in relation to the person's height, its movement around the person's body, and whether the flow is smooth or rough, but I don't see colors every time. I consider all of these elements and my intuitive impressions together as I do the reading. If you've ever had problems seeing auras, you may just see them differently than what is considered the norm. You may be like me and see auras in a different place than you'd expect it, which means they're manifesting in a way that is unique for you.

While color is connected with auras and is often seen in them, you may not see color every time, or you may never see color at all, so don't let this throw you off balance. Sometimes when I'm doing energy readings, I don't see colors but I do receive a wealth of information just from reading the energy flow. It's the same with auras. You might see color most of the time, but sometimes you're only seeing that white line around the person or no color at all, even though you're receiving a lot of information for them. And this is the key factor with aura readings: it's all about the information stored in the aura, which you will receive using your clair abilities. As an intuitive, you can access your clair abilities to help the person whom you're reading.

During an aura reading, you may obtain information about the person's health, personality, flaws, and positive traits; you may sense connections to past lives or information about their future based on the energy of the aura. When you're trying to see the aura, let your eyes go a bit out of focus as the subject stands or sits in front of a white background. You may only see the aura briefly in the beginning. You can also psychically sense the aura if you're having trouble seeing it. Tune into the subject's energy and see if you can psychically pick up the aura information and any color associated with it. Don't get discouraged if you're not seeing the aura right away. If you're having problems seeing it with your physical eyes, then look with your third eye or look in different areas than around the outside of the person.

Now that you know what auras are and ways to see them, you need to know how to use your intuitive ability to balance your aura. When your aura is out of balance, you'll feel out of sorts. You may be irritable, frustrated, and full of tension. The aura has several layers and when you're balancing it, you need to address each of these layers separately so that you bring balance from the inside out.

To balance your aura, you'll use your intuitive abilities to look inside yourself, examine your aura, and then use creative visualization to repair and strengthen it. This can be done in just a few minutes and you'll see quick results. As you examine your aura, you'll look at it on four different levels. First, look at your physical aura: do you see holes in it, areas that you can strengthen and reinforce? Next, look at your emotional aura. If the energy field surrounding your emotions is weak and unstable, it can have a negative effect on the other aspects of your entire aura. Now look at your mental aura for any hidden stresses or mental exhaustion. Finally, look at your spiritual aura for any areas of weakness. If you're having problems coping with a situation or if you're questioning your beliefs, you might find imbalances.

Try It Now: Balance Your Aura

Take the following steps to balance your aura. Sit quietly and intuitively look inside your being at your mental, spiritual, emotional, and physical energy, all of which make up your complete aura. Using creative visualization, open your crown chakra at the top of your head and imagine divine white light entering your body through your crown chakra. Let the white light fill you, starting at the core of your being and moving outward through all layers of your energy and aura. As white light fills every fiber of your being, allow it to push out any negativity you're holding on to while it's repairing all weak points of imbalance within your energy. As this white light moves to the outer physical part of your aura, allow it to go past the point of your own energy; then imagine it coming back on itself and creating a bubble around you, sealing you inside. All the negativity has been pushed out and you're protected from it. Your aura is now repaired, in balance, and filled with positivity.

Once you've balanced your aura, you will find that you're more creative, more emotionally stable, have less tension and stress, and are happier overall. A balanced aura will allow you to be one in mind, body, and spirit, which allows you greater stability as you work to enhance your intuitive abilities. A balanced aura allows you to see the world as it is; life is clearer, more defined, and has a smooth flow.

Energy Healing/Balancing/Distance Healing

Energy healing is the intuitive ability to manipulate the body's energy to bring about balance, clear negativity, and repair problem areas. It is using energy to affect energy. There are many popular methods of energy healing, such as acupressure, acupuncture, energy-focused body work (massage), Healing Touch, Reiki, and a plethora of different systems. Each of these methods has their own uniqueness that makes them different from one another, but at the core, the practitioners of these methods all use their intuition to connect to the energy of the person receiving the work to bring about balance and positivity. While most types of healing energy work dictate that one person does the work for another person, that doesn't mean that you can't do energy work for yourself.

During a session, the practitioner connects to Universal Energy, also called the Universal Life Force, through intuitive means, either through the third eye, connecting with spirit guides, or by seeing the aura. Once connected to Universal Energy, they often use their hands to transfer this energy to the person they're working with, sometimes by touching them or by holding their hands slightly above the person's body. Practitioners can focus energy in certain areas that feel disturbed, clearing where there are obstructions in the energy flow.

When it comes to energizing and healing our energy, I believe that there are times in our lives when we learn more about ourselves and need the connection that another person can give us. I also believe that it's important to know how to do this for ourselves. Learning how to use your abilities and your connection to your soul essence to repair your energy is a step forward in your growth. So how do you do it?

Start by finding time when you're not going to be interrupted, when you can devote an hour (or even thirty minutes if that's all the time you can spare) to examine and balance your energy. You can do this exercise either sitting down or lying on a bed or couch—just make sure you're comfortable. If your clothes feel constricting, put something else on. You don't want to have distractions around you, nor do you want to have distractions in your mind. The next step is to clear out all of those nagging thoughts so you're focused only on your energy. Now, feel yourself connecting to Universal Energy and feel it moving all around you. If you feel that you need your guides to help you, ask them for their assistance.

As this energy flows over you, intuitively look at your soul essence energy to find areas that feel weak, unstable, or empty. When you find these areas, imagine the Universal Energy flowing into them—strengthening, stabilizing, and filling them. Once you've examined your entire energy field and made corrections with the Universal Energy, you will feel more centered and balanced. At the end of the session, thank any guides who helped you and disconnect your intuitive senses from the Universal Energy.

Prayer is one of the most widely used forms of distance healing regardless of religion or belief system. *Distance healing* is when an intuitive senses the energy of a person who needs healing, and through the use of white light and positive intention they send healing energy to this person over any distance. You may send it to someone sitting right beside you or someone on the other side of the world.

You can help others by sending distance-healing energy when they are in need. When it comes to distance healing, each one of us is fully capable of using our intuitive abilities to connect with white light, give its energy a specific healing purpose, and send it to the person who has requested it. Sometimes intuitives do distance–healing sessions over the phone. While you may be hundreds or even thousands of miles apart, the session can take place during a phone conversation. This is energy work, therefore distance is not a barrier in achieving results. Distance healing can be used to help resolve specific problems, balance chakras, conduct Reiki sessions, clear karma, and help improve medical conditions.

We can send healing energy to help someone, but since we can only heal ourselves on a soul level, it is up to the recipient of the white light energy to use it in the way that feels right to them. As spiritual beings, we are solely responsible for our own health and mental well-being. That is why we should seek medical attention when we are sick and pay attention to our personal frequency and emotional health. During times of need, we can also ask others to send white light and healing energy to us. You can be both a sender and receiver of distance healing, which will help you heal emotionally and in mind, body, and spirit.

Try It Now:
Send White Light to Someone Needing It

For this exercise, you'll ask someone who may be going through a difficult time if you can send white light to them. Explain that they can use it for whatever purpose they need. Focus on the person and their energy, then imagine a ball or flowing ribbon of positively charged white light going from you to them. When you feel that the light has reached them, release it. After you've sent the white light, talk to the person again to find out if they felt it when you sent it to them.

Shell Hearing

During a vacation at the beach, you picked up a shell, put it to your ear, and heard the roar of the ocean waves within the shell. If you took the shell home, hundreds of miles from the beach, you'd still hear the ocean. Conch shells seem to work the best because of the spirals within the shell. Now cup your hand over your ear. Do you hear the slight roar of the ocean? It is believed that this sound is caused by the noises in your surroundings that are picked up and resonated through the shell of your cupped hand. You can also obtain the same effect with a plastic cup, coffee cup, or small bowl.

This is the basis of the ability called shell hearing. As an intuitive person, when you hold a shell to your ear, you may hear more than just the roar of the ocean or the resonated sounds of your surroundings. You may also hear whispered words or a specific voice. Some believe that when you do hear a voice in the shell, it is your subconscious sending your own thoughts back to you. But what if it's the voice of a loved one or a voice of a different gender? This is when your intuitive abilities come into the picture. Just as it is easier for a spirit to contact you in your dreams when you aren't consciously blocking them out, it is also easier for a spirit to contact you using shell hearing because your focus is on the sound and not on blocking. Sometimes you are only able to tap into your ability with shell hearing when you have two large shells and hold them up to both ears at the same time. Covering both ears seems to magnify your intuitive ability to tune in to whomever is trying to contact you using this method.

You can use shell hearing with the intention to contact your guides. Always protect yourself with white light before attempting any type of spirit contact, to keep negative entities at bay. Envelop yourself with white light before putting the shells, cups, or your hands over or close to your ears; ask that only positive, higher-level guides speak with you, and that negative, lower entities be kept away. Ask your guides to deliver any messages when you listen to the sound. You may hear whispered words or a spoken message; then again, you may not. I believe you'll only receive a message if you're supposed to receive one, regardless of how intuitive you are. So if you don't hear anything other than the roar of the ocean, that's fine. You can always try again later. Just know that you can use this method and your abilities to receive messages from your spirit guides.

Scrying

Scrying has been used by intuitives for a very long time. *Scrying* is when an intuitive stares into an object in order to receive visions. You do not have to use an object to receive visions—many clairvoyants never use scrying. If you find that you're having difficulty connecting to your clairvoyant ability, then you might give this a try.

When scrying, you can use a variety of objects. You've probably seen the picture of a psychic staring into a crystal ball, but this isn't the only way to accomplish your goal. You may decide to use a glass filled with water, the flame of a candle, any pool of water, smoke or fog, a bowl filled with water that has been darkened with ink, crystals, or the typical crystal ball. There is also the scrying mirror that has a black face instead of being reflective. Most metaphysical shops carry tools for scrying. The specific type of tool you use isn't important; it just has to be something that feels right to you. If you try one tool and it isn't working for you, try another one. If you're using a crystal, hold it in your hands until you feel it grow warm. This allows your energy to connect to the energy of the crystal. It is the same with the other tools, even if you can't hold them in your hand. You should feel a connection between your energy and the energy of the tool.

Some people prefer to conduct complete rituals each time they're scrying. They will do scrying in a dimly lit room with incense burning and music playing. While this practice is totally fine if it works for you, it is not the only way to be successful. You may be sitting on a park bench staring into the dark depths of a lake and start to receive impressions. Or maybe you're sitting at your office and have a glass of tea or coffee that you're drinking. You find yourself staring down into the cup at the liquid. Moments later you start to see a vision. Both of these are still scrying, just without the ritual.

The reason that the tool you're using isn't important, and the reason you can use a cup of coffee or a huge lake, is because you're not focusing on the actual scrying tool. You start by clearing your mind, finding your center, and relaxing your body. Then you can either wait for the visions to come or you can ask questions and wait for the answers. The purpose of scrying is to seek answers to a question for yourself or for someone you're reading. When you're scrying, you're looking past the tool. For instance, if you're using a flame, you start out looking at the flame but then your focus moves just past the flame. At this point you're connecting with your own clairvoyance and the visions will come. You will also use your intuitive ability to interpret the visions you see.

Divination

Divination is the "art or act of foretelling future events or revealing occult knowledge by means of alleged supernatural agency; to know by inspiration, intuition, or reflection" according to *The American Heritage Dictionary*. It is a broad term that includes clairvoyance, precognition, prophecy, card readings, runes, and other methods used in an effort to predict the future. Divination is when you use any tool or object during a reading, in addition to your intuition, to gain information that will help you in the present by understanding the past and looking into the future.

There are many different methods of divination that people use to foretell the future, to gain insight into current life situations, or to look into the past. There are methods of divination that read the moles on your body, the bumps on your head, and even the shape of dung. Some methods of divination are thousands of years old and aren't practiced anymore, others are rarely practiced, and some other methods are very common in modern-day use.

Divination can show situations in your life and possible outcomes for those situations. If you don't like what you see during your divination reading, or what is seen on your behalf, you can always change it because you have free will and the ability to make choices that affect your life path. Using divination tools along with your intuitive abilities allows you to see where you've been, where you are right now, and where you're going. The path you take is entirely in your hands. Using divination tools will help you focus when doing a reading.

Some of the different types of tools used during divination readings are tarot cards, runes, pendulums, oracle cards, scrying bowls, the I Ching, crystals, divining rods, and tea leaves, to name a few.

Try It Now:
Divination Reading with Playing Cards

You can try a divination reading right now using a regular deck of playing cards. Take the deck and shuffle well. As you're shuffling, think of a situation that needs clarity for you. As you think of this situation, cut the cards into three piles. Turn over the first card, knowing it represents the past situation. Now write down the impressions you receive about the situation when you turn that card over. When you're finished, go to the second card, which represents the present situation, and do the same thing. Next, go to the third card, which will represent the future or possible outcome, and repeat the process. Now look back at what you've written down. Do you see any seeds of truth in your words and impressions that will help you with your situation? Doing this type of reading allows you to connect intuitively with your guides and higher self to receive information that will help you resolve the situation.

Animal Communicator

An animal communicator has the intuitive ability to communicate with various kinds of creatures in the animal kingdom. This is also called *animal telepathy*. Someone with animal telepathy may picture something in their mind that they want the animal to do, send the picture to the animal, and ask it to follow the instructions, and the animal does it. This ability is quite often used in training animals and trainers often refer to it as a *technique* instead of an intuitive ability. (I believe it is an ability and not a technique.) It's easier for the animal to understand and learn if you're telepathically sending it visual images along with your verbal instructions. As an animal communicator, you will feel a special connection with animals. You will have a healthy respect for them but no fear. When you ask animals questions, you see, feel, or hear their response in your mind or you may even see visual images that they've sent back to you.

People who are animal communicators can help you resolve issues with the animals in your life. They are different from animal trainers in that they are not trying to train the animal to do something but are trying to understand why they are acting in particular ways.

Try It Now: Animal Communication

If you have a pet, you can try animal communication with it. If you don't own a pet, practice animal communication with a wild animal, such as a bird or squirrel. Send a thought and mental picture to the animal of something that you would like for it to do. If it's your pet, ask them to come to you when they're in a different room. If it's a wild animal, ask that it comes closer to you or that it moves in a certain direction. When you're practicing animal communication, make sure that you send the animal a visual image of what you're asking in addition to the thought in words. Write down your results and over time you'll find that your success rate increases.

Animal Totems

An *animal totem* is an animal spirit that guides you during your lifetime. Some animal totems are with you from birth to death, and others come and go in your life when you need them, just as some spirit guides do. Animal totems are all positive beings. If you find yourself encountering an animal in your dreams or an animal that evokes fear when you see it, there is something in your life that you need to change and the animal totem is there to help you change it.

Animal totems are not chosen by you; instead, they choose you. If there is a particular animal that you feel drawn to your entire life, it is probably a lifetime animal totem for you. For me, it is a horse. If there is an animal that has started to suddenly appear in your life, then its presence has meaning at that time. You'll become aware of this happening because the animal will get really close to you or will appear out of the blue. Today as I walked toward our tack room, I heard the beating of wings inside. In the years that we've had the barn, we've never had a bird fly inside the tack room. So I waited a minute, and a black raven flew out, right past me, and then went and perched on the side of one of the turnouts and stared at me. When I got home I looked up what a raven animal totem meant and discovered it is the keeper of secrets, heightened awareness, greater understanding of consciousness, and teacher of mysticism. All of which had meaning to me that day.

Take time to notice the animals around you, even if you don't own a pet. Pay attention to the animals you feel drawn to. Take the time to learn about them, what other cultures think about them, and their meaning as an animal totem. By learning about the animal, you may just learn something about yourself.

Try It Now: Connect with Your Animal Totem

For this exercise, I want you to find somewhere that you can sit comfortably or lie down. Close your eyes and ask that your animal totem come to you. It doesn't matter if you don't know the meaning of the animal totem; you can look it up later. The important aspect of this exercise is that you make the connection. Relax your body and clear your mind. Wait for your animal totem to appear in your mind's eye. When it does, don't be quick to reject it, especially if it is an animal that you don't like. Watch how the animal interacts with you as the scenario in your mind's eye plays out. Can you receive a message from what you're seeing? When the animal totem leaves, thank it for visiting with you and then look up what that particular animal means as a totem to you.

Master Palmist

A master palmist is someone who has studied and mastered the art of palmistry over many years and is able to read a person's character or predict their future by reading the lines and shapes in that person's palm(s). You do not need to be intuitive to be a palmist, but many people who read palms often use their intuition while doing the reading.

When a palm reading is conducted, there are many factors that are examined including the lines of the hand, the mounts, the shape of the fingers, the thickness of the hands, and the texture. Through these shapes, lines, and other qualities of your hands, the master palmist can often tell you about your life lessons and purposes, your challenges and potentials. They can predict the number of children you will have, your financials over your lifetime, and your spiritual path. A master palmist can also tell you about talents that you may not realize you have, how you respond to others emotionally, and how to find harmony in your relationships.

If you're interested in palmistry, you can learn to read the hands of other people through practice and further reading.

Past Life Regression/Past Life Consultant

If you've known how to do something that you shouldn't because you've never studied or practiced it, then you're probably connecting to a past life memory. Or maybe the first time you visited a place, you knew exactly what you'd see around the next corner. Do you have a phobia that has no root source in your current lifetime? All of these instances are signs of reincarnation.

Reincarnation is the belief that your soul has lived before in another physical body, time, and place. It is also the belief that when you die, you will go to the Other Side to review your life lessons to determine what you learned or didn't learn in your most recent lifetime, and then you'll be reborn into another body to learn the lessons that you still need to accomplish on your spiritual path. In each incarnation, you have the same soul, but different personalities. People you knew in past lives will often be part of your current life in order to work out any lessons between the two of you.

Being psychically attuned to your past lives can be very enlightening and can help you resolve situations that are holding you back in your current lifetime. I've done many past life readings for people and one emotion that always seems to come up is fear. You may be afraid of something in this lifetime that has its basis in a past lifetime. For instance, a fear of heights may be due to death from falling off a cliff three hundred years earlier. When the connection is made between the past life and the current fear, the person usually gets confirmation in the form of the Chills of Universal Truth or a sense of knowing they've experienced a soul truth. As a result, the fear usually dissipates immediately or relatively quickly thereafter.

Sometimes you may experience glimpses of past lives. We breed Friesian horses, and one of the horses, when I first met her, immediately put her head over my shoulder and breathed a big sigh. I looked at my husband and said, "This is my horse." Then one day, when I was mucking the turnout attached to her stall, I glanced over and she was in the doorway, standing tall, looking out across the field at the cars on the interstate. I immediately saw a glimpse of a past lifetime in which she was standing in exactly the same manner and I was cooking some kind of meat over a fire built inside a circle of rocks. I knew I was male in this past lifetime and it was during the medieval era. There was no doubt in my mind that she truly was my horse.

When you intuitively sense flashes like this, don't be too quick to think that it's just your imagination. Right after I saw this flash, my horse looked over at me, walked into the turnout, and nuzzled my face. That was all the confirmation I needed that what I'd just seen was real. This is called reliving a past life. While what I saw in this instance was just a glimpse, you can also remember an entire past life in complete detail.

Past life regression is when you use hypnosis to help you remember past lives so you can get to the root of current problems or discover more about yourself on a soul level. When you choose to follow this path, make sure that the person doing the hypnosis is a qualified professional with a lot of experience so that you don't get harmed in the process.

If you have ever wondered if you've had a past life and want to know about them without going through a hypnotically induced past life regression, then you can have a reading with a past life consultant. This is a person who is intuitively able to see your past lives by focusing on your energy.

Having a past life reading can enable you to overcome fears, see karma at work, learn life lessons, and make a connection to your soul essence. If the consultant is able to read emotions in addition to seeing events during the past life consultation, they can help you understand the feelings based in the past lifetime that may have remained and are still connected to you in your current lifetime.

A past life consultant can not only read your past lifetimes, but can also use their ability and intuition to help you resolve issues they saw in your past lifetimes. For instance, when I do a past life reading, I always ask why I was shown this lifetime and what the lesson is for the person I'm reading. Obtaining this information during the reading helps the person to resolve current issues.

Card Readers: Tarot, Oracle, and Animal Card Readings

Tarot cards have been around for thousands of years. They are most often used to connect with the higher self and receive insights about specific questions or general situations. Most often, the questions or situations are approached in a positive manner; you're asking for broad insight through the cards, posing a specific question or an answer before you even do the reading. For instance, if you're asking a question about your love life, you would ask how you can bring more love into your life instead of asking who you're going to marry. By asking the questions in this manner, you'll receive a more meaningful reading.

All tarot card decks consist of seventy-eight cards that include the major arcana and minor arcana. The major arcana are picture cards that represent ideals, principles, or concepts. Some of the card names (depending on the deck) are the Sun, the Moon, the World, Strength, the Lovers, Justice, and the Wheel of Fortune, to name a few. The minor arcana includes four suits: wands, swords, cups, and pentacles. Some decks substitute circles for pentacles. Each of the suits includes the king, queen, knight, and page, as well as numbered cards from one to ten.

Each tarot card has a specific meaning by itself and another meaning if it is laid upside down in the spread. A card can have additional meanings based on the other cards around it in the spread. Two of the more popular spreads are the Celtic cross, where the cards are placed in the shape of a cross and give an in-depth reading, and the three-card spread, where three cards are drawn that tell you the past of the situation, the situation now, and the future outcome.

Oracle cards are decks of cards that are used for divination. There is a wide variety of oracle cards that you can choose from when doing a reading for yourself or others. These decks can help you find answers to specific questions or give you a general overview of a situation. They can offer guidance or clarity about your life path and purpose. These cards can have many different themes. Some of the more popular types of oracle cards are angel cards, ascended master cards, animal totem cards, fairy cards, life purpose cards, and spirit guide cards. When selecting a deck for yourself, choose a theme and deck that you feel drawn to. By doing this, you have a connection to the cards and will choose one that will give you valuable information when you do a reading.

Once you've decided on the oracle cards and before you start using them, cleanse them and give them the purpose of working for the greater good. If at any time you feel that the energy of the cards is clogged or not flowing freely, then cleanse them again with white light. Using a variety of oracle cards can offer you different perspectives depending upon the theme of the deck. You may use one deck for your reading and another for further clarification of the same situation.

An animal card reading is when an intuitive uses an animal card deck to do an intuitive reading for you. These types of readings can be helpful to find your animal totem or to see how animals connect to you on a soul level. These are often called animal oracle readings or animal totem readings. People will often seek out animal readings after having a particular animal feature portrayed prominently in a dream or when a specific animal keeps appearing in their lives.

Tarot, oracle, and animal card readers use a combination of their intuition and clair abilities along with tarot cards, oracle cards, animal cards, or any of the many types of divination decks available to give a reading. These readings are done based upon the way the cards are cut and laid in a variety of spreads that give the reader insight into the person and the situation for which they are seeking guidance.

Each type of reading is used in a way that is specified by the instructions accompanying the particular deck. Some tarot or oracle card readers will allow the person for whom they're reading to choose the deck from which they want a reading to be conducted; other readers choose the deck they are drawn to when focusing on the person's energy.

When doing a tarot or oracle card reading, the reader will focus on the person and their situation, shuffle and cut the deck until it feels right (or have the person they're reading do this if it's an in-person reading), and then draw the cards, laying them out in the chosen spread. Then they interpret the spread according to the meaning of the cards and the intuitive impressions received. These types of readings can answer specific questions or give a general overview of a situation.

Try It Now:
Do a Tarot or Oracle Card Reading

If you already own a tarot or oracle card deck, then choose the deck you'd like to use for the reading. If you don't own a deck, then go to your local bookstore or online retailer and purchase one in order to do this exercise. When making your selection, choose one that you feel drawn to as detailed above. You can often glean more information if the deck comes with an interpretive book, so this may be an added option that you'd like to consider. Other decks come as complete sets with the deck, book, carrying case or bag, and a journal to log your results. You might prefer this type of complete set.

Once you have your deck, begin by doing a reading for yourself. Start with a simple three-card spread and focus on one specific question or situation. Shuffle the cards until you feel that the energy is right, and then cut the cards into several piles. Choose the piles you feel drawn to and then select a card from the top of each one or stack them back together and choose the first three cards from the top of the deck. Now read the meaning of each card and consider how it relates to your situation. Allow your intuition to give you additional information as you read about the past, present, and future of the situation. When you are finished with the reading, determine whether you've received a solution to your question.

Runes

Runes are an oracle that uses an ancient Germanic alphabet inscribed on tiles, small rocks, stones, or wood. Today, you can buy runes that have the symbols inscribed on metal, crystals, or plastic as well. These same symbols were used in writing thousands of years ago and were often found carved into standing stones, along well-traveled paths or roads, to guide travelers.

A rune reading is not a way to predict the future. When doing a rune reading, you will find that they can offer advice that makes you think and analyze your situation and a possible outcome. If you're intuitive, when doing a rune reading, you will rely on your intuition to help you clearly see what the runes are saying.

When casting runes, you will focus on your situation, then reach into the bag holding the runes and touch the various tiles until you feel that one connects with your energy. You remove that tile and lay it down in the pattern of the chosen spread. You continue doing this until all of the places in the spread are cast with a rune, then you follow the order of the spread and read the meaning of each rune from the accompanying instruction book. When interpreting the cast, you consider both the individual meaning of each rune and its position in the spread.

Rune casting can be very enlightening, especially when you're at times of change in your life.

....

Were you successful in meeting your guides or finding spirits on film? Did you meet your animal totem? This is just the beginning of a giant step in your path of enlightenment. As you recognize and learn to communicate with those on the Other Side and on other planes, you will become more aware of the vastness of the Universe. There is much that you can learn from these beings if you're open to their assistance.

Doing readings is an enjoyable way to practice using your intuitive abilities. Even if you're only doing them for yourself, you can gain insightful and wise knowledge through a variety of readings. Keep exploring your own abilities and trying different types of readings to find what works best for you. You may prefer one type over another to gain insight to questions and aid in spiritual growth. The knowledge you gain from readings is priceless.

Eight

✦

Types of Intuitive Communication

✦

Just as there are many types of guides and spiritual beings on the Other Side, there are also many ways that these entities can communicate with you. In this chapter, we're going to look at some of them. This is another section where I'd suggest you write down the messages received during communication. Being able to look back at your experiences is invaluable in your spiritual growth.

Afterlife Communication

Afterlife communication is the intuitive ability to communicate with people we have known on earth after they have returned to the spiritual plane; it is sometimes referred to as "after-death communication." During after-life communication, you'll often use several different intuitive abilities all at once. It is not uncommon to be able to hear messages, see mental pictures of the person as they appeared on earth, see souls in their spiritual form, or just know the message being delivered. The difference between this intuitive ability and other forms of contact with spiritual beings is that you are specifically connecting to people you have known on the earthly plane in this lifetime instead of spirit guides, angels, or masters.

When our loved ones pass, they often use signs to show us that they are still around and to express their love for us. It is their way of letting us know they're okay while we're grieving. Signs often appear when we're going about our daily activities. If someone you love has recently passed, you oftentimes will not receive messages from them right away. Your grief may be too intense and they may wait until more time has passed, if they choose to contact you at all. Other times, they will make their presence known during these times. Not all spirits will choose to communicate with the living, but when they do, it truly is a gift. When my grandmother passed, I was distraught. Then I heard my name in a song on the radio, a song that I knew for a fact didn't contain my name. One of the lyrics of the song was "I love you" and my name was inserted right before that lyric. I immediately received the impression of my grandmother smiling at me. A spirit oftentimes will connect with you through songs on the radio, sending you a message exactly when you need to hear it. Another day I was overwhelmed with grief and felt as if someone grasped my shoulders and hugged me. I sensed my grandmother nearby and didn't doubt for an instant that it was her way of letting me know that she was okay and that she loved me.

You can also experience afterlife communication with your animals. I've had this happen many times in my life, but the first time was so amazing that I never questioned the spirit realm again. I was just a little kid and my pony was shot and killed by hunters. I was in the pasture, lying down with her filly, when a strong wind came up the path from the creek. The filly was immediately on alert and jumped up, as did I, because it was a very strange wind. I heard my deceased pony neigh and the filly bolted from my side and took off down the path, following the wind, which changed direction and went back the way it had come, with the filly following. All I could do at the time was stand there, crying and smiling at the same time, while I was completely overcome with a feeling of wonder and amazement.

Animal Communication

You've probably heard the terms "pet psychic" or "animal communicator" used to describe clairvoyants who can telepathically converse with animals. If you own an animal, you've probably experienced, on some level, mental communication with your pet. Ever wondered where your dog or cat is, and the next moment they show up beside you? Subconsciously, you have telepathically called your pet to your side.

Animals know when you love them, like them, are afraid of them, or hate them. Their behavior will often reflect your feelings toward them because, either knowingly or unknowingly, you telepathically project those feelings to them. They may react in the way you expect due to your feelings about them, or they may act in a completely opposite manner. Let's look at two examples. A dog that senses you hate it may become defensive, raising the hair along its back and barking if you move toward it in an aggressive manner. That same dog, if it senses that you love it, will act submissive or try to play with you if you make those same aggressive moves. A horse that senses fear in a person will either remain calm itself to calm the person's fears or it will resort to its natural flight instinct and move away from the person.

You can use animal telepathy with intention to communicate with any animal. Wild animals are perfect test subjects to use as you strengthen this ability. Trying it on your own pet can be difficult because you already communicate telepathically with your pet. To do this exercise, take a trip to your local park, or if you live in the country, find some squirrels, birds, ducks, or any other wild animal. Start by sitting quietly and watching the animal. It doesn't matter how close or far away it is; you just have to be able to see it. Now, purposefully send the animal a thought. You may ask the animal to come closer to you, to change directions, or to do something very specific (for instance if it's a squirrel in a tree, you may ask it to come out of the tree). This would be a good time to keep a journal or log to see how many times you're successful with your communication attempts. If you do keep a log, you'll notice that over time you are more and more successful.

After you've become accustomed to communicating in this manner, the next step is to clear your mind and listen for any thoughts that may be coming from the animal to you. This can be a little harder. With practice, the impressions will become very clear and you'll pick up on them instantly. Soon you'll be able to communicate with all types of animals.

Silent Communication

There are times in your life when you may want to talk with someone who is unable to respond to you. In these situations, you will use your telepathic ability and clairvoyance to communicate with them. Some specific examples are an infant, someone who is far away from you, someone who isn't answering the telephone, or someone who is temporarily unable to speak for some physical reason (they may be asleep, in a coma, etc.).

When you need to communicate with someone who doesn't have the ability to respond, the first thing you should do is quiet your mind. If it's a loved one who is injured, this can be difficult to accomplish because your emotions are running high. Before you attempt communication, it's important that you rise above your emotions and are at a level of high vibration, love, light, and calm solitude. Imagine a path of energy between the two of you on which your thoughts will travel. Open yourself to your intuitive abilities so that you will be able to receive their responses. If you're upset or overly emotional, those feelings can block your ability to receive impressions. Calmly send your thoughts to the other person and listen for a response.

Trying to communicate with someone who can't verbally speak may be frustrating if you're not grounded and centered before you attempt contact. Imagine yourself surrounded by silence, then fill that silence with white light; if you fill the white light with your love for the person you are speaking with, you will be more successful. Later, you just may find out how much they understood and how accurate your impressions were. It's important to maintain a positive, grounded energy around you because this will help their words come through without bombarding them with overly emotional noise.

If we all are more aware of our intuitive ability to communicate with others in this manner, then we can share our love with those currently unable to physically talk to us.

Someone Calls Your Name

Ever heard someone call your name, turned around to look, and no one was there? When hearing a voice is related to intuition, it often happens in the same way every time. You hear someone say or shout your name, and while it feels as if the voice is coming from outside of you, as if someone else is calling you, it also sounds as if it's right beside your ear. It sounds both far away and nearby at the same time. When I've heard this, it always seems as though the sound is coming from above and slightly to my right side. You may experience this during the day as a loud shout, but it can also happen just as you're falling asleep or as you're waking up because you're more receptive to contact during these times. I've noticed that when this happens to me, it's because my spirit guide has a message for me and I'm very busy or I'm just not actively being aware of my guides. My name is called to get my attention so the message can be delivered. This also happens when guides have messages I'm supposed to deliver to other people. When I hear my name called in this manner, I no longer look to see if someone is there because I know it's my guides trying to make contact.

If you've heard your name called, first pay attention to see if it's your guides. Your guides will often contact you in this manner when it's important and you're not paying attention. Other times, you may feel that the voice is coming from a less-pure energy source than the energy of your guides. There are many instances where the voice is thought to be from a ghost or lower-level spirit. Because you don't want these entities calling out your name, ask your guides to protect you from this kind of contact and ask that they are the only ones who can communicate with you by calling out your name. Anytime you're dealing with situations that are paranormal in nature, you should always protect yourself with divine white light so that lower energies stay away from you. If you do this, then when you experience your name being called, you'll know, as I do, that it's from a positive, divine source and not a negative, lower-level source.

Mass-Media Messages

Let's pretend you're driving down the road, lost in thought about a problem you're presently trying to solve, and you notice a message on a sign that seems to apply to your situation. Perhaps you're having a relationship issue and you're feeling angry, stressed, and underappreciated. You see a billboard for an air conditioning company that says, "Relax in cool comfort today." Moments later, you notice another billboard that says, "Speak now, we'll listen." Next, you see another that says, "Pick your battles." What is going on here?

First, you're sending out negative energy into the Universe because you're upset and worried about the problems you're encountering in your relationship. This is normal human behavior because we all get upset sometimes. Things don't always go the way you expect them to, people give you a hard time, and you allow this negative energy to affect your mood. Your guides pick up on this energy and send you reassuring messages and helpful ways to resolve the issue. You just have to be intuitively in tune with the energy around you to understand what you're sensing. In this example, these messages are telling you to relax—if you do, you'll cool down and find comfort. Speak now—it's time to talk out the situation with your loved one; if you try this approach, you will be listened to. Instead of trying to have everything your way, pick your battles. By following this advice, you may just discover that your situation is resolved and you're no longer stressed or upset but happy again.

Sometimes when things are going badly, we can block our intuitive abilities without realizing that we're doing so. By paying attention to mass-media messages, you are removing the block, tuning into your abilities, and comprehending the help that is being sent from your guides. Mass-media messages can come from many sources, including television shows, radio programs, billboards, and advertisements and commercials. You just have to pay attention to the information received when it seems to jump out at you like this.

One way you can use your intuitive abilities to your advantage when you're experiencing less than positive situations in your life is to ask for help. Tune in to your clairvoyance and ask that you're shown the way to correct the problem with the least amount of effort. Then, pay particular attention to the world around you. When the message is there, it will stand out in some way. You may only catch a phrase, or it may be a longer message. When you hear it or read it, you'll immediately feel a connection to those words that just seems "right" and you'll know the course you should take. By paying attention intuitively, you are more aware and can make conscious choices and decisions based on the messages you receive.

Open a Book at Random to Receive a Message

There are books on the market that are made with the purpose of random fortune telling. To use them, you'll think of a question, intuitively focus on the answer to your situation being shown to you in the book, and then open the book to a random page and read the message printed there. I have several of these books and they're fun to use and have been oddly accurate in the advice given. You just have to make sure that you're focused on the question or issue at hand prior to opening the book. If you're not focused, you may end up doing it over and over again and then you'll end up confused and frustrated. Using these books in this method is similar to doing a one-card reading with tarot or oracle cards. It gives you a brief overall insight into the situation with which you need help. Just make sure you're not doing it over and over because you don't like the first message. Think about its application to your situation.

If you've ever felt yourself drawn to a bookstore or library when you really didn't need or want to visit one, then you should heed this feeling because it's usually guidance from the Other Side. Your spirit guides will have a message for you in that bookstore. This happened to me recently. I had to go to the bookstore to pick up a book for my son's reading class. I walked in the front door and right there in front of me was a huge stack of books with the same title minus one *s* as one of my novels. I continued to the kids' section and felt drawn to a particular row. There on the shelf, facing out, was a book with the name "Cassandra" on it. Well, I had to laugh at that point and ask what the message was because I just wasn't getting it. You see, Cassandra is my primary life guide who has been with me since birth. It took a couple of hours for me to understand that particular message but it did become clear soon after the event. To add another layer to this experience, the only reason I was at the bookstore that day was because I'd already bought one copy of the book my son needed and it had simply disappeared somewhere in our house. Is it all connected? Sure it is. The missing book turned up later.

There are plenty of times when you're in a bookstore or library and you suddenly feel compelled to pick up a specific book or to visit a section that you normally wouldn't visit. If you feel it, do it. Open the book you feel drawn to and just look at the page. See if any words seem to jump out at you, giving you a message that, if you think about it, will apply to an area of concern in your life or will give a message of hope and inspiration. I've even seen a book on the shelf and when I went to pick it up, it wasn't there. Well, that was so bizarre that I called a psychic friend who felt I was seeing a book that I would write in the future. It made sense so I'll just wait to see if that specific cover ever develops for one of my books.

The Veil

When it comes to your intuitive abilities, you'll discover that they continually grow and strengthen. Things that you may never have thought about but have experienced will one day become suddenly very clear. For years I've seen a misty white substance similar to smoke, vapor, or a cloud and would then receive an intuitive impression, but I never associated this mist with anything. I just thought it was one of the ways I received impressions. Then, not too long ago, I was working at the farm, giving one of my horses some water, when I looked to my right and saw what looked like a huge, misty, white cloud of smoke low to the ground. It looked as if it were a living thing, moving in a swirling motion, not a normal movement for a cloud of smoke, so I thought there was something wrong with my vision. I blinked a few times and the cloud was gone. I went out into the yard and looked around and couldn't find any evidence of a cloud, white mist, smoke, or even a fire. Later that day I stopped by the bookstore, opened up a book at random, and read about how the veil between this world and the Other Side can appear as a misty white substance or as a cloud. I'd been aware of my abilities for years, I knew about the veil between this world and the Other Side, but for some reason I'd never realized before that day that the white mist I see is the actual veil itself. When the time is right, the information will come. You'll always continue to learn in this field regardless of the length of time you've been involved with it.

Music

Each soul has a song. Have you just started humming some tune that you've never heard before but it touches you on a soul level? It feels as if it comes from the depths of your soul; it feels real and true. You think about it, trying to place where you've heard it before, but realize that you just can't place the tune. This soul song is one that you'll find yourself humming over and over again throughout your life, because it is your song, the essence of your being coming alive through music. You have intuitively reclaimed a bit of your true essence when you connect to your soul song.

Just as you can intuitively connect to the music of your soul, you can also use music to increase your abilities. Listening to different types of music will empower your intuitive receptors. You'll discover that if you open to your abilities as you listen to music, you will be able to see impressions more clearly; you'll feel the ebb and flow of the music and empathically feel messages. When you connect to music, it is also easier for your guides to reach out to you.

Finding the right type of music is important. You may choose different types of music based on the abilities that you are trying to utilize. If you're trying to connect to the spiritual realm, then you may select music that is ethereal and light. Or, if you're trying to increase your empathic abilities, you might prefer a strong, deep song that really gets your emotions going. Sticking with instrumental pieces is the best when developing your abilities. Sometimes words just get in the way of what you're trying to accomplish. You may find yourself listening to them instead of the flow and beat of the song. You want to feel the music, connect to it intuitively, and allow its rhythm to affect you.

Sometimes music is the tool used to get you to focus on your guides or departed loved ones. They'll send you messages through the words of songs. When you're trying to further develop your abilities, try different types of instrumental music to see which works best for you.

Try It Now:
Listen to Music to Connect to Your Intuition

Make sure you've allotted some quiet time where you can listen to music without interruption. As you listen, pay attention to both the piece as a whole and the individual instruments that make up the song. Don't try to think logically, but instead look clairvoyantly, feel empathically, and listen not only with your ears but with your clairaudient abilities as well. When you've finished listening to the selections, don't immediately jump up and start doing something. Instead, take a few minutes to notice anything you may sense intuitively. Are you getting messages from your guides? Seeing a future event? Or do you suddenly know how to resolve a situation? Music is an excellent tool to attune to a higher frequency, thus increasing your intuitive abilities.

Repeating Numbers

When you see repeating numbers, pay attention to what you're thinking at the time and what is going on in your life. You may be seeing numbers like 11:11, 222, or 1515. Whatever the numbers are, you see that number repeated over and over again. Just the other day, I was buying shovels at a store and when I checked out the clerk said, "That'll be $44.44." I immediately said, "What?" because I'd seen 444 a couple of times earlier in the day. She repeated the total and told me that I should play the lottery that night, which goes to show you that people in general think repeated numbers hold some kind of importance, even if they don't know what it means. When numbers show up in repetition and in multiples during the day, then it is a sign for you. You are intuitively receiving a sign from your spirit guide or your higher self. There are several excellent books on the market that give you meanings for these numbers. Not every author will give the same meaning to each number, but you can read these to get an idea of what other people think. However, you should always look at your own situation to determine what this number means in your own life.

People may say that it's just coincidence when this happens. Logical thinking would suggest that because you see so many numbers during a day, your mind fixates on the repetition. I can see that point. But I also know that I don't notice repeating numbers every day. When I do see them and they make me pause, I become very aware of them. It's almost as if I'm supposed to notice them. The other day our power was out due to a storm and every time I looked at my cell phone or a battery-operated clock, it was 11:11, 1:11, 4:44, 5:55, etc. I was really uptight and on edge that day and had a lot of different unexpected things going on: First, we lost power, so the extreme heat in the house meant I could only write in longhand. Next, a dog needed stitches. Then, a horse's eye was infected and needed treatment. I kept thinking, *I've got to look that number up*, because it is always helpful to read what others think the messages are for repeating numbers. Later that day, after seeing these numbers many times, I realized it didn't matter what anyone else said the numbers meant; to me, on that day, they all meant "calm down, everything is going to be okay." Once I got that message clearly in my mind, I didn't see any more repeating numbers. I did calm down and everything was okay.

Be aware. Look at what you're going through, your emotions, and the way you're thinking about your situation. Notice the numbers, look them up, and then apply what you've read to what you empathically feel or clairvoyantly sense to discover the message held in repetitive numbers.

....

By now you should be feeling a true connection to your intuitive abilities, your guides, and those on the Other Side. You are probably using your abilities daily to assist you and make your life easier. Keep up the great work and continue to always research and learn more about your abilities and your spiritual self. This is part of your spiritual growth. You are connecting to your true soul essence by delving into this part of your being.

Nine

Protecting Yourself from Negative Situations

While no one likes to talk about negative things in life, there are times when they should be addressed. I've tried to give you a very positive approach to learning about your abilities and the development of those abilities. However, because the world is full of both positive and negative energy, I've also included some of the things you should watch out for in this chapter.

Psychic Vampire

Psychic abilities are based in energy. We all have a life force, a personal frequency, and spiritual energy. The higher these levels are, the more in tune you are with your intuitive nature and Universal Energy. While we all have intuitive abilities, a psychic vampire is a person who uses their abilities to drain the energy of surrounding people, thereby increasing their own energy levels.

We all have the tendency and ability to drain another's energy. You do not want to become a psychic vampire because using your abilities in this way is negative and impedes your spiritual growth. While we all have relied on someone else's energy during times of need, hardship, or despair, this is not the same as intentionally drawing energy from those around you on a regular basis so that you feel better. People who drain energy from others subconsciously usually aren't even aware of what they are doing.

How can you tell if you're a psychic vampire? There are certain characteristics associated with people who tend to drain another's energy. They may be needy and require constant nurturing from everyone around them, feel like they always have low energy, need the approval of others, are never satisfied with what they have in life, and are always wanting more and more. They often feel alone, as if no one cares about them. When you encounter people like this, they connect to you, drawing on your energy stores, and you walk away feeling as if you've been run over by a truck and could sleep for a week, while they are bubbling over with energy. That's because they drew from your energy while you weren't paying attention. A psychic vampire can give you an instant headache, make you feel like you can't think straight, or cause you to be irritable and feel bad all over. Sometimes these symptoms will disappear when you're no longer interacting with these people, but other times they can linger and only a good night's sleep can balance your energy flow.

Try It Now:
Protect Yourself from Psychic Vampires

To protect yourself against psychic vampires, you can carry or wear quartz crystals and you should always protect yourself with white light. As you pay attention to those who drain your energy, you can make sure to specifically protect against them, too. You may even be able to help them see what they are doing if they don't realize it, and teach them to use their abilities for positive work. Often there is a self-esteem issue going on with a psychic vampire. Just make sure that if you're going to try to help them, your energy is well protected from their draining effects. You should also remove any negative connections that psychic vampires attach to you. Look for them on your body and use creative visualization to cut them loose or pull them out of your energy field. Then put up a protective barrier of mirrors on your bubble of white light so that no one can reconnect to your energy.

Psychic Attack

Human nature being what it is, there are people who thrive on pessimism, who expect that only bad, undesirable things will happen to them, who always see the glass as half empty instead of half full. Because they view the world in this manner, if they embrace their abilities they tend to use them in a negative way, especially when they have feelings of anger, jealousy, or hate. You may, at some point in your life, even find yourself under psychic attack from one of these individuals. A *psychic attack* is when a person consciously and deliberately sends a negative and destructive telepathic thought or psychic attachment to another person with the intention of harming that person on some level and in some way. These thoughts and attachments are connected to the person's energy and frequency by entering through the aura. A psychic attack is also considered to be when a negative entity from the lower spiritual realms attaches itself to someone, through these same energy channels, causing disruption, out-of-character actions, and disturbing thought patterns in the life of the victim.

We all have fears within us that we haven't resolved by facing them. Psychic attacks are based in fear and usually target your fears, leaving you feeling on edge, helpless, and as if you don't have the power to change the situation. Psychic attacks can come from an individual or from a group. If you can eliminate the fear and replace it with love and compassion for the person(s) trying to psychically attack you, then your positive energy will overwhelm their negativity and they'll stop the attack. It's not easy by any means, because when you know someone is deliberately trying to harm you on a spiritual level, your first reaction may be to strike back. Just do so with positive energy and love instead of any kind of negativity.

Being intuitive yourself, you can easily use your abilities to defend against all types of psychic attacks once you learn to recognize the signs. The first sign to look for is anything that is out of line with your normal behavior and character. The second sign is fatigue. Because a psychic attack drains your energy, you'll feel tired—sometimes extremely so—even when you're getting plenty of sleep. Being in the presence of the person doing the attack will fatigue you very quickly. You may also experience headaches, extreme sleepiness, nightmares, negative thoughts, sudden chills (not the good kind), or shaking and trembling throughout your body.

Your intuitive self will often give you a warning when you're in a situation that could potentially turn into a psychic attack. You'll feel it as a tightening, sick feeling; if you don't act on that feeling, you'll start feeling fatigue as the person doing the psychic attacking drains your energy.

Try It Now: Eliminate a Psychic Attack

The best way to eliminate a psychic attack is to encase yourself completely inside a bubble of white light. You can empower it to great heights through creative visualization by adding a golden or blue tone and mirrors to increase the protection. Combine white light protection with love and compassion for the individual(s) attacking you. Ask your spirit guides to help you send the psychic attack back to where it came from. Use stones and crystals for protection, and use the power of prayer to end the attack. Sometimes you may have to get help from your intuitive friends if the attack is severe. Practice doing this so you'll be prepared if you ever need to use this method in a hurry.

Mental Influence/Psychic Manipulation

Some intuitives have the ability to use mental influence to manipulate objects or other people. While there is nothing wrong with using your ability in this manner to clear phone lines or open up parking spaces, I have a big problem with intuitives who try to use this ability to influence and manipulate other people. When you're using this ability to help you get through to a company whose phone is always busy or find a parking space in the middle of a holiday season, you're not harming anyone in the process. But when you use this ability to manipulate someone so that they will do what you want them to do, then you have crossed an ethical line.

We all have free will and we all have intuitive ability. It's important to learn how to detect people who are trying to bend your will to theirs through the use of their ability. If you find yourself suddenly thinking out of character and in a way that might help someone else, stop what you're doing and wait. Cleanse your energy with white light and put the intention of protection around you, reinforcing it around your mind. Do you feel a shift, as if you've released something from your energy? Do you no longer want to follow through on the help you were just about to give? If any of these things are true, then you have effectively stopped an intuitive manipulator from using their ability of mental influence on you.

On the other hand, if you're using your mental influence to manipulate the energy of a person to help them clear their energy or find balance, with their permission, this is different. Why? Because you have their permission and they know what you're doing; you both agreed what would happen when the person sought out your help. In this instance, you are still being ethical and trying to help the person. If you have this ability, always use it for the good of others instead of trying to bend another person to your will and desires.

Another form of psychic manipulation that I want to mention here is intuitives who try to instill fear in you in order to get you to spend more money with them. They may tell you that they do all sorts of wonderful work, but can't prove any of it. They may hint at horrible things coming your way, but in order for you to find out so you can be prepared, you must spend a gazillion dollars with them. Never give any psychic thousands of dollars for a reading. You can find all of the answers you seek by looking inside yourself and using your own abilities. If you really feel you need an intuitive to help you, find one who is reputable, honest, and operates with a statement of ethics. You should never feel that you have to depend on an intuitive for any reason. A legitimate intuitive will not allow you to become dependent on them but will help you help yourself, and they will not charge exorbitant fees. If you are doing readings for others, treat people as you want to be treated and be ethical in your practice.

Psychic Kinetic Energy

Kinetic energy is the energy of motion. When a person has abilities in using psychic kinetic energy, they involuntarily influence inanimate objects around them without having any physical contact. Instances of kinetic energy seem to be stronger during times of hormonal changes like puberty, menopause, or pregnancy, although it can happen at any time. It affects men, women, and children equally. The person who is affected by kinetic energy doesn't seem to be able to control it; therefore, it happens at random or sporadically. The person may affect objects daily for months, and then this ability disappears as quickly as it appeared. It can re-emerge in the future during times of stress or hormonal changes within the body. There are other people who have it consistently throughout life and it's especially apparent when they are around electrical or technological objects—they walk into your kitchen and the light bulbs blow and your microwave goes on the fritz!

The word "poltergeist" is often used to describe kinetic energy. Because there have been movies made surrounding kinetic energy manifestations and attributing them to hauntings, there can be confusion between the two. I personally do not think that poltergeist activity is in any way related to a haunting. Instead, you'll notice that the abrupt noises, bangs, movement of inanimate objects, audible voices, and the like only happen when a specific person is around. If that person is removed from the room, all instances of the "haunting" stop. Bring them back in and the "ghost" returns.

What causes these kinds of psychic kinetic energy activity? I believe it comes from people who have intuitive abilities, especially if they do not know they have them, or they are ignoring or denying their abilities. I see this happening with individuals going through emotional turmoil, high levels of stress, and those who do not express their feelings. I also believe that there are others who intuitively and spiritually operate at a very high frequency (personal vibrational rate) and can affect the things around them unconsciously. Of course, these people can put up blocks around them so they're not blowing every light bulb or street light they come into contact with, but it could still happen due to an overflow of their positive energy.

So what do you do if you are affecting the world around you in this manner? The first thing to do is to take stock of your intuitive abilities and your frequency levels by focusing on where they are; if necessary, bring them back to center and ground them. The next thing you do is address any emotional problems you're having—areas of high stress or frustration—and then try to reduce the stress levels or at least get them under control.

Acknowledge how your energy is affecting your surroundings and make a concentrated effort to keep your energy balanced within yourself so that it's not projecting outwardly. And lastly, understand that outbursts of psychic kinetic energy are usually random and temporary. They will pass. If you help yourself by learning about this phenomenon and understanding yourself, you can help them pass sooner than later.

A Grain of Salt: Don't Believe Everything You Hear

Psychic readings should never be blindly followed. You should always follow your own heart and your own gut instincts. You have free will and it's this free will and the decisions you make after you've received a reading that will alter your path. Just as there are many people who truly have abilities and want to help you, there are also people who want to rip you off and put fear in your heart. I've run across this many times. I've given away many readings to people because they've been scared to death from a previous reading they received and couldn't afford the amounts that the psychic said they had to pay to "fix them." No one should ever charge you thousands of dollars for readings, scare you, or take advantage of you like this, leaving you feeling like you don't know where to turn and frightened in the search for truth. Not only do these people give real intuitives a bad name, they work on your deepest fears in order to get you to buy more of their services. Don't fall for their scams. Don't pay ridiculous prices to anyone for a psychic service. Real intuitives will not tell you that something bad will happen to you if you don't purchase three thousand dollars of additional services. Be aware of the people who do these kinds of negative things and don't fall for it if it ever happens to you.

How to Recognize a Fraudulent Psychic

There aren't many things on this earth that get me upset because I believe we all have our own paths to follow and lessons to learn. I try to remain balanced and calm in my approach to life. However, sometimes, as hard as I try, situations can just crawl right up under my skin until I have to address them.

Once, while doing research online, I ran across a "cry for help" on a random message board. Without revealing the details, I'll give you an overview of the situation. A person was asking how they could help a family member who was being scammed by a psychic. This psychic was supposedly "curing" the family member of a major disease (that there isn't a medical cure for yet) and at the same time was trying to manage the woman's finances. A week prior to this incident, I heard of another similar situation where someone had lost five thousand dollars to a psychic and I saw on the news that a lady had given a psychic three hundred thousand dollars. That same week, I received a spam e-mail from a psychic saying she had information that I must claim within the next week by ordering a reading with her.

It's easy to get caught up in someone's hype when they are playing on your emotions, insecurities, and fears, but you have to be aware of what's going on around you and understand that, unfortunately, not everyone in this world is a good person with good intentions. Ultimately, you are responsible for your own life; while people can help and guide you, they can't fix all of your problems for you. If they did, how would you ever learn the life lessons that you came here to learn? You can't be scammed if you're aware that there are scammers out there and know how they work. If you've ordered a reading and the psychic just keeps saying you need more and more readings, that is a clear sign that they're not a legitimate, ethical psychic. Don't give them your money because taking it is their ultimate goal, not helping you. If they threaten you, contact the police.

It really saddens me when people take advantage of others this way, regardless of career. Don't let your desperation make you do things that you'd never do otherwise or trust people whom your gut is telling you to steer clear of. Listen to your own intuition.

You should never pay exorbitant amounts of money to someone who makes great claims that they can fix all of your problems. If it sounds too good to be true, it probably is. Be skeptical, and look for logical reasons for what the psychic says. Are they reading your body language? Are they asking you leading questions?

When getting an intuitive reading, there are certain responsibilities that both parties have in order to make sure you're receiving a good reading and aren't being ripped off. If you're going in for a reading, there are several things that you should do prior to handing over your hard-earned cash; additionally, there are things that you should never do. Let's take a look at them:

Always:

1. Read the intuitive's website from top to bottom. Ask questions about anything that is unclear. If they can't give you a clear answer without telling you that you need to order first, don't order from them.

2. Make sure the intuitive is upfront about their ethical practices.

3. Conduct an Internet search on the person. Look for any negativity about their site name or about them as an individual. If you find a lot of complaints, don't order from them. If you only find a couple, still consider the person as a potential intuitive to read for you because no intuitive is 100 percent accurate all of the time.

4. Ask for references. The intuitive should be able to put you in contact with someone whom they've read before so you can talk to them one-on-one.

5. If you're still not sure, ask if they will give you a sample reading, or buy a one-question reading and see what kind of answer you get before ordering a more expensive reading. If the intuitive is truly trying to help others, they shouldn't have a problem with giving you a sample first. But don't just ask for a sample to get a free reading. That's not fair to the intuitive either because they are giving you their time.

6. Ask the psychic what happens if they are wrong. Will they give a refund, even if they have a no-refund policy? Find out what the refund policy is before you order.

7. Are the psychic's rates reasonable or are you paying a gazillion dollars for a thirty-minute telephone reading or a one-hundred-word e-mail reading? There shouldn't be a limit placed on the reading, in my opinion. They should give you all of the impressions that they receive, even if it's more than what the reading you ordered covers. Sometimes you'll actually get a lot more than you paid for.

Never:

1. Don't be naïve when you go into a reading. Be skeptical until you see the kind of reading delivered to you.

2. Don't answer leading questions. An intuitive shouldn't have to ask you questions. If they do, don't answer unless it's a simple yes or no that lets the intuitive know that what they said was correct. If you feel uncomfortable even giving that much, just tell them you don't want to say anything until the end. They should be fine with that. Let them give you a reading,

rather than gleaning information from your answers so that they're just saying what they think you want to hear. When a psychic is working off of your feedback, it is called a "cold reading" and isn't really using psychic abilities.

3. Don't go into a reading expecting answers to all your problems. No psychic is 100 percent accurate, so don't necessarily expect to receive all the information you seek.

4. Don't believe that an intuitive is going to bring back your lost loves, cure diseases, or fix everything in your life if you pay them enough money. It's NOT going to happen. People who are telling you that they can do these things aren't being honest with you or with themselves.

5. Do not substitute a reading with an intuitive for a visit to your doctor. Go to the doctor. They're trained medical professionals and they can help you with your health problems.

6. Do not feel pressured by an intuitive. If they ever ask you to buy another reading (or buy a first reading) before they'll give information that they've already received for you, walk away. If the information was given to them, it was for a reason and they should relay it to you, whether or not you buy anything from them. When you see this happening, it's just the intuitive trying to make money. In my opinion, this is wrong.

7. Never, ever let an intuitive make any financial decisions for you.

8. Never, ever let an intuitive make health decisions for you.

9. Never, ever let an intuitive have any involvement with your children.

10. Take everything that the intuitive tells you with a grain of salt. Intuitives aren't all-knowing. They make mistakes and misinterpret information even if they aren't frauds. They're only human.

11. When it comes right down to it, it's all about ethics. Not everyone believes in intuitive abilities or the paranormal and it's a very controversial topic. It's hard to believe until you've experienced it firsthand, and even then it can be difficult. It is good to be somewhat skeptical to protect yourself from people who only want to take advantage of your situation.

Remember that while others can offer guidance, you (and only you) have the ultimate control over your life and destiny. Do not expect or ask a psychic to make decisions for you—that's not their place. It's up to you to make any final decisions regarding issues in your life. The decisions you make will allow you to grow on your spiritual path. Draw strength from positivity and light instead of delving into negativity and darkness. It's your life; live it to the fullest. People can only take advantage of you if you *allow* them to take advantage of you. Don't allow it. Be firm in your resolve; pay attention to what is going on around you. Be a participant in your life, not just an observer. Never allow yourself to be victimized by others. Be strong and powerful, and make educated choices by seeking answers before agreeing to anything.

900 Lines

Everyone has the right to an accurate reading at an affordable price by a reputable psychic who is centered and confident with their abilities. In my opinion, 900 numbers that charge you by the minute are only out for your money. The majority of people that I know appreciate being able to obtain accurate insight from a reputable source without paying an arm and a leg for their reading.

You've all heard about them; you may have even called them yourself (I have)—psychic hotlines whose phone number goes something like 1-900-***-****. While this is a profitable business, it's one that I don't suggest that you use. Why? Because *most* of the people working there are reading from a script, keeping you on the phone longer than necessary and running up a tremendous bill to ensure profit in their pockets and a big phone bill for you. Now, that said, please notice that I didn't say *all* of the people working there read from a script. I do know a few people who worked for these types of businesses who were truly intuitive and ethical and who worked there to earn extra money so they could make ends meet. But, in my overall experience, speaking of the 900-industry on the whole, this usually isn't the case.

Recently, a member of my family obtained a new job in a sales call center. At that job was another newly hired person who had just left a job as a "psychic" with one of these 900 facilities. He told my family member all about the book that he had to read from. They had to memorize different scenarios and then keep the person talking and on the phone so they could look up anything that they hadn't memorized yet. There was a specific answer that they were to give for specific situations. The person who worked there said the book was a huge training manual that they were to read from without sounding like they were reading. This really makes me mad because they're playing with people looking for help for pain and suffering in their lives, and reading suggestions from a book when the person is looking for a true intuitive reading is despicable and thieving, in my opinion.

....

Remember that no living person or spirit can affect you negatively unless you allow them to do so. Be strong; be sure of yourself and your abilities, and of your positive spiritual nature. Do not let fear or negativity become a large part of your life. When negative things happen, face them, resolve them, and move on. Dwelling on them only gives them your energy and the power to bring you down. Everything in life happens for a reason, and we all have lessons to learn. Let your lessons come, learn from them, and move on. You can't change the past, but you can always change your future.

Ten

Where Do You Go from Here?

Hopefully you've learned to recognize, develop, and embrace your intuitive abilities by reading this book. But where do you go from here? You keep reading, learning, and incorporating all that you've learned. I've listed some books that may interest you in the recommended reading list at the end of this book. Becoming spiritually enlightened is a lifelong journey. I truly appreciate that you chose to take a few steps of your journey with me.

Ethics and Responsibilities

Now that you've arrived at the end of this book, it is time to think about how all of this applies to you. Have you recognized abilities within yourself that you didn't realize you had? I hope so! Have you thought about how you will use these abilities? Each and every ability you have enables you to learn and grow spiritually. Here are a few options to consider as you decide how you will continue to grow.

Some of you may only want to use your abilities for yourself, to help you in life and on your spiritual path. Others of you may decide that you would like to use your abilities to do readings for your friends and family. Or, you may decide that you have developed your abilities to the point that you would like to do professional readings for the general public. Any of these choices may be the right one for you based on how you feel about your abilities and where you are on your spiritual path. You may start out only using your abilities for yourself, but in a few years you may be at the point where you're ready to do professional readings.

Whichever path you choose, there is one thing to keep in mind: always be ethical, honest, and responsible in your dealings with others and with yourself. Treat others the way you'd like to be treated, and be honest and open, especially if you're working with the general public. Be transparent; help others along the way by giving more than you're receiving, because in doing this, not only are you helping someone else, you're making great strides along your own spiritual path.

The Challenges and Joys of Working as a Professional Intuitive

Working as a professional intuitive can be both an inspiration and a challenge. Let's look at the challenges first. There are days when you may encounter people who are blocking you when they request a reading, whether intentionally or unintentionally, and it is more difficult doing a reading when your customer is blocking you than if a customer is open to your reading. There are other times you may encounter someone who has been scammed by an intuitive who has put fear in their heart, and it will be your job to alleviate this fear and set their hearts at ease so that they are no longer afraid. Sometimes you may see loss or things that are difficult to see and that you might not want to know about, but you're being shown the information for a reason. As a professional intuitive, you have to learn how to deal with the situations that arise during a reading and deliver the information in a tactful, caring manner.

Not everything about being a professional intuitive is a challenge, though. It is the joy received that makes all of the challenges worthwhile—the joy in knowing your insights have been helpful to someone, that you've made a difference in their lives, that you've helped them through a difficult time. When you see a pregnancy for someone who has been trying but hasn't gotten pregnant yet and you get a vision of a little girl, and then a year later the mother sends you a picture of the child who looks exactly as you envisioned her—well, that is a precious gift and one of the great joys of this line of work. When you can help someone release their fears through understanding a past life, it is miraculous. When something you say connects to someone on a soul level, enabling them to grow spiritually and see themselves as their core being—there are no words to express how fulfilling that is. When someone's pet runs off and you give them a direction in which to look, then they e-mail you back to say they found the pet in that direction, well, these are some of the reasons that I keep doing this work. And these are only some of the joys which truly abound as you work as a professional intuitive, helping others realize their fullest potential as the spiritual being they are at their true soul essence.

Remember that as you walk this path of enlightenment, you do not walk it alone.

Recommended Reading List

Akashic Records

Insightful and enlightening, a must for your personal library—
Todeschi, Kevin J. *Edgar Cayce on the Akashic Records: The Book of Life.*
Virginia Beach, VA: A.R.E. Press, 1998.

Everyone accesses the Akashic Records differently. This book is an
excellent guide for those who want to learn how to read the records—
Howe, Linda. *How to Read the Akashic Records: Accessing the Archive of
the Soul and Its Journey.* Boulder, CO: Sounds True, 2010.

Angels

A must-have reference book for the meanings of angel numbers when
you encounter them in your life—
Virtue, Doreen. *Angel Numbers 101: The Meaning of 111, 123, 444, and
Other Number Sequences.* Carlsbad, CA: Hay House, 2008.

An excellent resource about connecting with the angels and also how
to work with them in your own life—
Steiger, Brad. *The Big Book of Angels: Angelic Encounters, Expert Answers,
Listening to and Working with Your Guardian Angel.* New York:
Rodale, 2002.

Animal Communication/Animal Totems

Not only does this book teach you how to communicate telepathically with your animals, but it also teaches you how to use Reiki to help in healing them—

Murray, Steve. *Animal Psychic Communication Plus Reiki Pet Healing*. Las Vegas, NV: Mind and Body Productions, 2009.

Lists and details a wide variety of animal guides and totems—

Farmer, Steven D. *Animal Spirit Guides: An Easy-to-Use Handbook for Identifying and Understanding Your Power Animals and Animal Spirit Helpers*. Carlsbad, CA: Hay House, 2006.

Astral Projection/Astral Travel

Practical advice and exercises that teach you to visit the astral plane—

Bruce, Robert, and Brian Mercer. *Mastering Astral Projection: 90-day Guide to Out-of-Body Experience*. Woodbury, MN: Llewellyn Worldwide, 2004.

Fascinating, down-to-earth guide that teaches how to astral travel—

Buhlman, William. *Adventures Beyond the Body: How to Experience Out-of-Body Travel*. New York: HarperCollins, 1996.

Auras

Excellent advice on energy and the aura—

Ambrose, Kala. *The Awakened Aura: Experiencing the Evolution of Your Energy Body*. Woodbury, MN: Llewellyn Worldwide, 2011.

A good guide that discusses the colors associated with auras and their meanings. This book was actually written by Cayce himself and isn't very long, only about twenty pages, but full of information—

Cayce, Edgar. *Auras: An Essay on the Meaning of Colors*. Virginia Beach, VA: A.R.E. Press, 1973.

An excellent how-to guide that is great for beginners and experienced aura readers. Step by step instructions that will guide you to seeing the auras of others—

Andrews, Ted. *How to See and Read the Aura.* Woodbury, MN: Llewellyn Worldwide, 2006.

Chakras

To learn more about the chakra system and the method of divination I invented—

Alvarez, Melissa. *Chakra Divination® Cards and Charts Activity Book.* West Palm Beach, FL: Adrema Press, 2010.

An outstanding book that teaches you how to use a variety of tools to awaken your chakras—

Lembo, Margaret Ann. *Chakra Awakening: Transform Your Reality Using Crystals, Color, Aromatherapy & the Power of Positive Thought.* Woodbury, MN: Llewellyn Worldwide, 2011.

Channeling

Informational book that discusses various ways to connect with your guides through channeling—

Roman, Sanaya, and Duane Packer. *Opening to Channel: How to Connect with Your Guide.* Tiburon, CA: H.J. Kramer, 1987.

Highly rated, informative, and offering step-by-step instructions targeted at beginners—

Coffman, Betsy-Morgan. *I'm Beside Myself!: A Beginner's Guide to Channeling.* Albuquerque, NM: Gabriel Light Publishing, 2008.

Creative Visualization

Excellent resource and easy-to-understand guide—

Gawain, Shakti. *Creative Visualization: Use the Power of Your Imagination to Create What You Want in Your Life*. Novato, CA: New World Library, 2002.

This is a good resource to use when you're just starting to learn about creative visualization—

Webster, Richard. *Creative Visualization for Beginners*. Woodbury, MN: Llewellyn Worldwide, 2005.

Divination

The go-to book about divination in the marketplace. Highly recommended—

Cunningham, Scott. *Divination for Beginners: Reading the Past, Present & Future*. Woodbury, MN: Llewellyn Worldwide, 2003.

Dowsing

A great resource for beginning dowsers—

Webster, Richard. *Dowsing for Beginners: How to Find Water, Wealth, and Lost Objects*. Woodbury, MN: Llewellyn Worldwide, 1996.

Use this book to take dowsing to a more spiritual level—

Lonegren, Sig. *Spiritual Dowsing: Tools for Exploring the Intangible Realms*. Glastonbury, Somerset, UK: Gothic Image Publications, 2007.

Dreams

One of the most complete encyclopedias for dream interpretation—

Chung, Theresa. *The Element Encyclopedia of 20,000 Dreams: The Ultimate A–Z to Interpret the Secrets of Your Dreams*. New York: HarperCollins, 2006.

A great resource for interpreting your dreams—
Zolar. *Zolar's Encyclopedia and Dictionary of Dreams: Fully Revised and Updated for the 21st Century*. New York: Fireside, 1963.

Elemental and Nature Spirits

A must-have reference book if you're working on understanding the paranormal—
Cheung, Theresa. *The Element Encyclopedia of the Psychic World: The Ultimate A-Z of Spirits, Mysteries, and the Paranormal*. New York: Harper Element, 2006.

Interesting discussion of the author's experiences with a wide variety of nature spirits and elemental beings—
Pogacnik, Marko. *Nature Spirits & Elemental Beings: Working with the Intelligence in Nature*. Forres, Scotland: Findhorn Press, 2009.

Energy

A year's worth of exercises that will help you raise your personal vibration—
Alvarez, Melissa. *365 Ways to Raise Your Frequency*. Woodbury, MN: Llewellyn Worldwide, 2012.

Great advice for helping you to create positive energy in your life—
Whitehurst, Tess. *The Good Energy Book*. Woodbury, MN: Llewellyn Worldwide, 2012.

Good resource to help you understand the different forms of energy medicine—
Thomas, Linnie. *The Encyclopedia of Energy Medicine*. Minneapolis, MN: Fairview Press, 2010.

Lucid Dreaming

Offers practical advice from a scientific point of view—

Laberge, Stephen. *Exploring the World of Lucid Dreaming*. New York: Ballantine Publishing Group, 1990.

Excellent guide for anyone who wants to learn lucid dreaming—

McElroy, Mark. *Lucid Dreaming for Beginners: Simple Techniques for Creating Interactive Dreams*. Woodbury, MN: Llewellyn Worldwide, 2007.

Manifesting

An excellent resource that teaches you how to manifest by using the law of attraction—

Byrne, Rhonda. *The Secret*. New York: Atria Books, 2006.

Experience the law of attraction from the viewpoint of a channeled spirit—

Hicks, Esther, and Jerry Hicks. *The Law of Attraction: The Basics of the Teachings of Abraham*. Carlsbad, CA: Hay House, 2006.

Meditation

A good book that shows meditation doesn't have to take a lot of time to work—

Davich, Victor N. *8 Minute Meditation: Quiet Your Mind. Change Your Life*. New York: Perigree Books, 2004.

Practical advice to use mediation daily to obtain balance in your life—

Rofe, Rachel J. *Meditation: How to Reduce Stress, Get Healthy, and Find Your Happiness in Just 15 Minutes a Day*. Rachel J. Rolf, 2010.

Mediums

The title says it all. This book is very down-to-earth and is highly recommended for anyone who wants to develop their abilities as a medium—

Vanden Eynden, Rose. *So You Want to Be a Medium?: A Down-to-Earth Guide.* Woodbury, MN: Llewellyn Worldwide, 2006.

Inspirational biography of a medium as she recounts her own experiences—

Hancock, Maureen. *The Medium Next Door: Adventures of a Real-Life Ghost Whisperer.* Deerfield Beach, FL: Health Communications, 2011.

Near-Death Experiences

Scientific viewpoint of why near-death experiences happen and interesting stories of near-death experiences—

Perry, Paul, and Jeffrey Long, MD. *Evidence of the Afterlife: The Science of Near-Death Experiences.* New York: HarperCollins, 2011.

A scientific look at near-death experiences—

Carter, Chris. *Science and the Near-Death Experience: How Consciousness Survives Death.* Rochester, VT: Inner Traditions, 2010.

Palmistry

A great book on palmistry that contains lots of illustrations and photographs—

Reid, Lori. *Art of Hand Reading.* New York: DK Publishing, 1999.

A new method for reading palms that is simple and easy to do—

Fincham, Johnny. *Palmistry: Apprentice to Pro in 24 Hours; The Easiest Palmistry Course Ever Written.* Ropley, Hants, UK: O Books, 2007.

Past Lives

An amazing book that I recommend everyone read more than once—

Weiss, Brian. *Many Lives, Many Masters: The True Story of a Prominent Psychiatrist, His Young Patient, and the Past Life Therapy that Changed Both Their Lives.* New York: Fireside Books, 1988.

Just as the title says, this is a book that will empower you as you learn how to discover your past lives—

Linn, Denise. *Past Lives, Present Miracles: The Most Empowering Book on Reincarnation You'll Ever Read … in this Lifetime!* Carlsbad, CA: Hay House, 1997.

Psychic Development

A plethora of symbols interpreted and exercises for use in psychic development—

Barnum, Melanie. *The Book of Psychic Symbols: Interpreting Intuitive Messages.* Woodbury, MN: Llewellyn Worldwide, 2012.

Perfect for beginners developing their abilities—

Owens, Elizabeth. *Spiritualism and Clairvoyance for Beginners.* Woodbury, MN: Llewellyn Worldwide, 2005.

Understanding your psychic type can make using your abilities easier—

Dillard, Sherrie. *Discover Your Psychic Type: Developing and Using Your Natural Intuition.* Woodbury, MN: Llewellyn Worldwide, 2008.

A hands-on approach to psychic development—

Choquette, Sonia. *The Psychic Pathway: A Workbook for Reawakening the Voice of Your Soul.* New York: Three Rivers Press, 1995.

Psychic Protection

Learn to protect yourself from the negative energy that surrounds you—

Bloom, William. *Psychic Protection: Creating Positive Energies for People and Places*. New York: Fireside, 1996.

Filled with exercises, checklists, and methods for protection against negativity—

Matthews, Caitlin. *Psychic Shield: The Personal Handbook of Psychic Protection*. Berkeley, CA: Ulysses Press, 2006.

Remote Viewing

A great resource from a former Army Special Forces major trained in remote viewing by the CIA—

Morehouse, David A. Ph.D. *Remote Viewing: The Complete User's Manual for Coordinate Remote Viewing*. Boulder, CO: Sounds True, 2008.

Learn to quiet the mind through remote viewing—

Targ, Russell. *Limitless Mind: A Guide to Remote Viewing and Transformation of Consciousness*. Boulder, CO: Sounds True, 2008.

Runes

A must-have book if you're interested in runes and want to do readings with them—

Blum, Ralph H. *The Book of Runes: 25th Anniversary Edition*. New York: St. Martin's Press, 2008.

Learn to use the runes with this workshop approach—

Halls, Jennifer. *The Runes Workshop: A You Know Intuition Workbook*. Fort Mill, SC: You Know™ LLC, 2009.

Scrying

An excellent introduction to scrying—

Tyson, Donald. *Scrying For Beginners*. Woodbury, MN: Llewellyn
     Worldwide, 1997.

Contains a complete set of instructions to have you scrying in no time—

Hawk, Ambrose. *Exploring Scrying*. Franklin Lakes, NJ: Career Press, 2001.

Spirit Guides

A well-defined look at how guides work in the spirit realm—

Choquette, Sonia. *Ask Your Guides: Connecting to Your Divine Support
     System*. Carlsbad, CA: Hay House Inc., 2006.

Practical steps to learn how to connect to your spirit guides—

Browne, Sylvia. *Contacting Your Spirit Guide*. Carlsbad, CA:
     Hay House, 2003.

Synchronicity

An easy-to-read approach to synchronicity—

Surprise, Kirby. *Synchronicity: The Art of Coincidence, Choice, and
     Unlocking Your Mind*. Franklin Lakes, NJ: Career Press, 2012.

Learn to recognize the meaningful signs of synchronicity in your life—

Soliel, Mary. *I Can See Clearly Now: How Synchronicity Illuminates Our
     Lives*. Lincoln, NE: iUniverse, 2008.

Tarot

A good guide on how to read the tarot for beginning students—

Bunning, Joan. *Learning the Tarot: A Tarot Book for Beginners*. York
     Beach, ME: Red Wheel/Weiser, 1998.

Easy-to-understand tarot instruction—

Louis, Anthony. *Tarot Plain and Simple*. Woodbury, MN: Llewellyn
     Worldwide, 1996.

Bibliography

Bletzer, June G. Ph.D. *The Donning International Encyclopedic Psychic Dictionary*. West Chester, PA: Whitford Press, 1986.

Gibson, Walter B., and Litzka R. Gibson. *The Complete Illustrated Book of the Psychic Sciences*. New York: Doubleday, 1966.

Jack, Alex. *The New Age Dictionary*. New York: Japan Publications, 1976.

Matthews, John, and Caitlin Matthews. *The Element Encyclopedia of Magical Creatures*. New York: Barnes and Noble Books, 2005.

The American Heritage Dictionary: Second College Edition. Boston: Houghton Mifflin, 1982.

Websites:

http://science.howstuffworks.com/question556.htm
http://www.participatorystudyseries.com/prophecy.shtml
http://www.diviningmind.com
http://www.fas.org/irp/program/collect/stargate.htm
http://www.animaltotem.com/raven.html

GET MORE AT LLEWELLYN.COM

Visit us online to browse hundreds of our books and decks, plus sign up to receive our e-newsletters and exclusive online offers.

- Free tarot readings • Spell-a-Day • Moon phases
- Recipes, spells, and tips • Blogs • Encyclopedia
- Author interviews, articles, and upcoming events

GET SOCIAL WITH LLEWELLYN

Find us on    @LlewellynBooks

www.Facebook.com/LlewellynBooks

GET BOOKS AT LLEWELLYN

LLEWELLYN ORDERING INFORMATION

Order online: Visit our website at www.llewellyn.com to select your books and place an order on our secure server.

Order by phone:
- Call toll free within the US at 1-877-NEW-WRLD (1-877-639-9753)
- We accept VISA, MasterCard, American Express, and Discover.

Order by mail:
Send the full price of your order (MN residents add 6.875% sales tax) in US funds plus postage and handling to: Llewellyn Worldwide, 2143 Wooddale Drive, Woodbury, MN 55125-2989

POSTAGE AND HANDLING

STANDARD (US):(Please allow 12 business days)
$30.00 and under, add $6.00.
$30.01 and over, FREE SHIPPING.

CANADA:
We cannot ship to Canada. Please shop your local bookstore or Amazon Canada.

INTERNATIONAL:
Customers pay the actual shipping cost to the final destination, which includes tracking information.

Visit us online for more shipping options. Prices subject to change.

FREE CATALOG!

To order, call
1-877-NEW-WRLD
ext. 8236
or visit our
website